Made by MORGAN

Morgan Hipworth started to dabble in the kitchen at age seven, and held his first Sweets and Treats home bake sale at age nine, before going on to sell his sweet wares to Melbourne cafes. In 2016 at age fifteen, Morgan launched his Windsor bakehouse Bistro Morgan. He lives in Melbourne and spends his days thinking about food, making food and enjoying food.

Made by MORGAN

MORGAN HIPWORTH

Contents

My Journey... So Far

My name is Morgan. Some of you might know me as 'that doughnut kid from Melbourne', but there's more to my story. Much more.

Food is my passion, and I am so proud to share some of my favourite recipe creations here in this book. I'm only just in my twenties but already I have what feels like a lifetime of experience in the kitchen. One of my favourite things is creating and mixing big, bold flavours that my tastebuds won't forget, but growing up I didn't know a cucumber from a zucchini (they look pretty much the same, right?). It's not that my parents didn't try to introduce me to interesting food – I was just an extremely fussy eater. I lived off chicken nuggets. Most of the time my mum threw them in the oven for my dinner, but on weekends I got a special treat: KFC nuggets. My parents loved going to a local Vietnamese restaurant, and the only way they could get me there without complaining was to pick up KFC on the way. There I would sit in this lovely little restaurant, surrounded by amazing sights and smells and the sound of sizzling stir-fries, tucking in to my takeaway nuggets while getting weird looks from staff and other customers. I look back now at my five-year-old self and I have to smile at the irony. (And of course I have included my recipe for chicken nuggets in this book. I wouldn't deprive you of that!) Needless to say, my palate has expanded considerably since those days, though I am still partial to the old classic fried chicken.

My childhood diet was as bland and boring as it gets. I stayed away from lollies and soft drink and all those other nasties, but I loved comfort food such as mac-and-cheese and burgers, and you'll see from the dishes in this book that I still love fun, tasty food that makes you feel happy. For me, that feeling of comfort and happiness is linked with my family.

I've always been close to my parents, and being an only child meant that I probably grew up a bit faster than most of my friends. My mum and dad encouraged me to form opinions and express my views freely from a very early age. This, I'm sure, has played a huge part in any success I've achieved in business and in life. In my home, determination was always a good thing. And I'm still just in my twenties – I've got a long way to go!

You might recognise my face (and my doughnuts) from when I was a guest judge on *Junior MasterChef Australia* in 2020, but my connection with the show started long before that – in fact, it's pretty much all thanks to *MasterChef* that you're reading these words right now. Early in 2009 I sat with my parents watching TV after dinner when a preview for *MasterChef* came on. At this stage I had been experimenting in the kitchen and gaining confidence, but I still vividly remember turning to my dad and saying, 'That looks *so* boring! Who would want to watch people cook?' But after some convincing on my dad's part, I watched the show – and it truly changed my life.

Watching *MasterChef* became an event in our family. Each weeknight we would gather on the couch to watch the next episode, and then on weekends I would re-create dishes from that week's elimination challenge – the more complex the dish, the happier I was. The following year, I applied for season two of *Junior MasterChef Australia*. I'll never forget the day my mum told me I had been invited to an audition. So many feelings and thoughts raced through my head – excitement, nervousness and a good dollop of self-doubt. I mean, I was only nine years old!

For the next two months I was a whirlwind, learning every new skill in the kitchen I could, and refining what I already knew. Then audition day arrived and I was a bundle of nerves. I took in my signature pavlova (see page 82), and met the other hopeful applicants. The casting directors interviewed us on camera and then tasted our dishes. We went through a few more rounds of tasks (my banana pancakes on page 14 were born from my *Junior MasterChef Australia* audition day), and then that was it – we went home to wait to see if we made the cut.

I was gutted to miss out, but I figured that if *Junior MasterChef Australia* wasn't going to happen, surely I could still make my cooking dream a reality – I would just have to do it myself. So, over the course of the next few months, that's exactly what I did.

A few weeks after my *Junior MasterChef Australia* audition, my parents and I went on a trip to the United States. We did all the typical tourist things – Disneyland, Statue of Liberty, Golden Gate Bridge – but the highlight was an epic French dinner at Bouchon Bistro in the Napa Valley on Bastille Day. I met Michelin-starred chef and owner Thomas Keller, and I left feeling incredibly inspired and determined. When we arrived home in Melbourne I surprised my jetlagged parents by turning our dining room into a restaurant. I printed menu cards, set the table and cooked all day. My main dish for the night was steak frites, and to this day that dish holds a special place in my heart. (See page 26 for my version.) I named my 'restaurant' – you guessed it – Bistro Morgan.

Over the next three years, Bistro Morgan became the main focus of my life. Each weekend I would go all out to impress my family. I still loved French food, but over time my palate and my passion for different culinary cultures meant I experimented, though often I came back to my favourites of French and Asian. I was lucky enough to do a fair bit of travel with my parents, and every trip involved amazingly different foods and led me to experiment and expand my repertoire.

These Bistro Morgan dinners led to a new idea: 'Sweets and Treats' days in our garage. I invited everyone I knew, and I baked for days. Guests could 'dine in' with a coffee from our Nespresso machine, or they could take the goodies away. I loved that my Sweets and Treats days brought people together, as food should, but it was also the first time I sold my food in a retail-like setting. It was the beginning of an idea that would one day come to fruition.

Once I realised that the food world consisted of more than chicken nuggets, I became desperate to try everything the Melbourne food scene had to offer. Because if you're a foodie, what better place to grow up? Fortunately, my parents were more than happy to come along on these culinary adventures. On one of these outings I got chatting to the owner of a cafe, and from this I got my first gig supplying my favourite sweets – vanilla slice, cookies, muffins, tarts, cakes and brownies (at this point I had never made a doughnut) – to Hawk & Hunter in Ripponlea. I vividly remember the day in January 2015 when Mum drove me and my first carload of sweet goodies to Hawk & Hunter: it was stinking hot and I spent the whole trip worrying that my vanilla slice was going to melt – but with the aircon blasting, everything stayed intact. After a highly successful first outing, my business was off to an incredible start.

Bistro Morgan was officially born. I registered the business name, and with the help of my ever-patient and supportive parents, my career began. It wasn't easy, but I was determined to do it. The cafe would place its order each day at 4 p.m. This meant I could be at school until 3.30 p.m. and then come home to start baking – sometimes until the early hours of the morning – while juggling homework and trying to get a bit of sleep.

My parents have always been super supportive of everything I've done, but looking back, this was next-level support, and I will forever be grateful. Being a year-nine student while starting a side business was a huge commitment. My mum and dad had to wade through all sorts of red tape to ensure our home kitchen met government requirements, plus there was the not-small matter of sourcing (and paying for) all my ingredients and equipment, and physically delivering the baked goods on time to the cafe. Mum and Dad bought the ingredients for my first wholesale order (I still have the receipt!). From that first order I made around $20 profit, which I used to buy my next set of ingredients, and then so on and so forth until I made enough profit from each order to put a little bit away as savings.

For Valentine's Day, Hawk & Hunter requested something special. I love a challenge, so I set my mind to it and made my very first batch of doughnuts. I tried out the recipe during the week, and roped some friends in as taste-testers. I am pleased to say, they were blown away! The customers loved my heart-shaped doughnuts, and over the next couple of months I tweaked the recipe until I came up with the one that we still use to this day. (I have shared a recipe for doughnut dough on page 100, but it's not my secret one – that would take way too long. This one is a more manageable version for you at home.)

From that day onwards I made doughnuts every weekend – my customers couldn't get enough! I started with simple flavours – vanilla custard, lemon curd, salted caramel – then I experimented with more adventurous offerings. Thanks to the manager of Hawk & Hunter, I also discovered what would become a signature feature of my doughnuts: a syringe with which people could inject their own filling. These syringe doughnuts became so popular that I gradually phased out my other sweets and focused on my doughnuts. (As a side note, I no longer use syringes, because I aim to avoid single-use plastics as much as possible.)

My business started to attract attention through our Bistro Morgan Instagram account, and before long I was supplying more cafes and holding market stalls; each time my doughnuts were a winner. But an interview I did in the *Herald Sun* was the springboard to my business becoming what it is today.

One morning, before I had even seen the interview in the newspaper, my phone started to beep with notifications, the most notable a DM from a producer on *Today* asking me to fly to Sydney to appear on the show. As if that wasn't surprising enough, all of a sudden I had calls from TV shows and radio stations asking for interviews – all while Mum and I were doing our usual early-morning cafe deliveries. I was excited but overwhelmed. Soon we had film cameras following us on our morning deliveries and then heading back to our house to film me making doughnuts. Before I knew it, it was lunchtime and I realised that in the chaos of it all I hadn't rocked up to school!

My very first live TV appearance was the weirdest feeling. I helped set up the fifty doughnuts I had stayed up till 3 a.m. baking, and before I knew it I was being broadcast live on Channel 9's breakfast TV show. On the way home, my Bistro Morgan Instagram account ticked over 1000 followers, and the phone buzzed non-stop. The media frenzy exploded the business – in a week I went from supplying two cafes to more than twenty, with another thirty on a waiting list – and things started to get seriously busy. My life consisted of school, homework smashed out in the library during recess and lunch breaks, then home to focus on the business. My weekends were all about doughnuts: we would churn out between 500 and 800, and I would create around fifteen new flavours every week. Over my two years of supplying all those Melbourne cafes, I made around 1000 flavours, all while completing years nine and ten at school. By this stage, my mind was made up about the next step I wanted to take in my baking and business journey . . .

My parents were strongly against the idea of having a permanent store, but I was determined. I wanted my own place, somewhere I could sell my doughnuts directly to the public. I had proved my determination and willingness to work, as well as my burgeoning business sense, so in 2016, after many arguments, we settled on a compromise: I would hold a pop-up store during the school holidays. I knew exactly what I wanted, and I found an amazing space on High Street, Windsor, just off Chapel Street.

It was the most insane week of my life. Each day I started to bake at 4 a.m. and finished in the store around midnight. We had a constant line of customers out the door – over eight days we sold more than 10,000 doughnuts. On the final day, *Sunrise* did a live cross to us, and this led to an invitation from David Koch to come to their Melbourne live cross that Friday for the AFL Grand Final, which of course I jumped at, because if you have ever lived in Melbourne you will understand just how massive a day it is for the city.

After the success of my pop-up, my parents were closer than ever to letting me have a permanent store. After many 'discussions', we took on the lease in late 2016, as I was finishing year ten. It was a significant financial investment to get the shop up and running, and it drained every dollar I had saved, but I knew it would be worth it. By this stage I had realised that though I retained the name Bistro Morgan, I wanted this space to be a bakehouse. Sweet treats were what I loved most, and that's what we focused on: doughnuts, cookies, scrolls, toasties, coffee and shakes.

Around the same time, I did work experience with the producers of *Today* in Sydney. The experience taught me a lot – from the importance of organisation to social and digital marketing, and about the connection to an audience when marketing a product. For me this has always been really important, because I want people to know that there is a story behind my business.

On my final day the producers offered me a segment to announce the opening of my permanent store, and of course I said yes. The next morning I announced on live breakfast TV that Bistro Morgan Bakehouse would officially open its doors. There was no getting out of it now!

The grand opening was surreal – I finally had what I had dreamed of for so, so long. It was, however, a little weird when I went back to school the next year – I would sit at my desk thinking, *Oh my god, right now Mum's selling my doughnuts in my store while I'm sitting here in English class.* This novelty quickly wore off, lol.

Over the next eighteen months, the bakehouse prospered amid ongoing media coverage, while I had my head in the books getting through year eleven. Heading into year twelve, I didn't slow down. During this crazy year I also put myself through the most intense experience of my life: appearing on TV again, this time on *Shark Tank*. My parents and I thought long and hard about our strategy. I was never desperate for a deal, but at the same time I knew that if I was made the right offer by the right shark, I would take it. My main concern was to not lose too much control of the business and its direction.

With Mum and Dad

In March 2018, Mum and I flew to Sydney with some doughnuts for the sharks to try. As I marched from the green room into the tank and was greeted by the four sharks, I was more intimidated than I have ever been in my life! But I took a deep breath and composed myself, ready to make my pitch. I spoke for forty-five minutes and then endured half an hour of intense questioning from the sharks. I received two offers, but both stipulated too high a percent equity, and it was a straight no from me. Though I didn't end up getting the deal, shark Janine Allis kindly offered me a mentorship, which has been invaluable, and I know I made the right decision to continue running my business my way.

After I finished school, things got real. I worked full-time in the business, plus had many other adventures. In 2019, I held a pop-up store in a Los Angeles bakery, my doughnuts so sought after that people drove two hours from San Diego to LA for them; it was an insane feeling to be on the other side of the world and have people flocking to grab these things. From this came a whirlwind of opportunities, including hosting a TV miniseries on Nick Jr, where I created Nickelodeon-themed doughnuts and taught kids how to make them. It was crazy – not so long ago I was the kid learning how to cook, now I was teaching others!

I've had some amazing opportunities – and I hope to have many more – but one of the most memorable so far was serving as a guest judge on the 2020 series of *Junior MasterChef Australia*. It brought back all the memories of my time as a hopeful applicant. Going back as a judge made me stop and appreciate just how far I had come in not an especially long time. It was an honour and so much fun to share my story with the amazing kids who were on the show. And their cooking! I was blown away by the skill these kids showed.

I have always loved sharing my food and experiences, and social media in recent years has allowed me to connect with an audience and (I hope) inspire people to get into the kitchen. It is so rewarding. I love it when kids come into the bakehouse and chat to me, because once upon a time I was that kid who wanted a start in the food industry. If I can give them any advice about getting into the kitchen or on a path to what they want to do, then I've done my job for the day. When I look back at the people who have influenced my culinary journey so far, I appreciate each and every one of them, and it is really nice to pay it forward when I can.

Well, that's my story so far. I might have been known as the doughnut kid, but through this book I want to show you that I am much more. And I'm not finished yet! Not nearly. I have so many more plans and dreams, but in the meantime I hope you enjoy the recipes I share here – it's the food I cook for my family and friends. Start a conversation over the food, watch your loved ones smile as they enjoy what you've created and, most importantly, enjoy the process of being in the kitchen. I'm there with you all the way!

FOR FLAVOURS
BISTRO
MORGAN
BISTRO
MORGAN

BISTRO
MORGAN
Seriously Good Doughnuts
BISTRO
MORGAN
Seriously Good Doughnuts

BISTRO
MORGAN

BISTR
MORGA

My Cooking Style

When I'm in the kitchen, for the most part I trust my instincts. When I was starting out, though, I had to follow every recipe to a T. I used to get so frustrated when something didn't work exactly the way I wanted it to, which is funny because back then, things rarely went according to plan. When I was nine, I thought I was king of the kitchen, and I decided to make a pavlova with zero help. I somehow misread '2 teaspoons white vinegar' as a whopping '2 cups white vinegar'. I put the pav into the oven and then left it to cool overnight . . . you can imagine how badly the house reeked of vinegar the next morning! What followed was tears, tantrums and a very bruised ego. At the time it felt like the worst day of my life, but it taught me to always double- then triple-check the recipe, especially when making something for the first time. I could go on and on about the countless mistakes I've made along the way, but it really is the only way you learn and progress. So, embrace the stuff-ups! One important thing to note if you are just starting out on your cooking journey is to be super careful in the kitchen, particularly with hot surfaces and foods; things can become dangerous if you don't follow directions and use equipment correctly. In particular, a few of my recipes involve hot oil for deep-frying – make sure you have an experienced cook in the kitchen with you as you learn to navigate around hot oils.

The more knowledge and experience I gain in the kitchen, the more I realise the importance of knowing what I am trying to achieve. Now, I taste along the way, add flavours and adapt as I go. The recipes in this book are written to my taste and how I like them, but keep in mind that we all have different tastes – there's nothing wrong with adding or adapting these recipes to suit your taste. I don't want you to stress – I want you to enjoy making an amazing dish.

Growing up, I loved the fine-dining experience, the theatre of a degustation menu and all that jazz, but these days I prefer something simpler. I don't want to have to trek around to specialist food shops and spend a fortune on obscure ingredients – I think it takes so much of the fun out of food. And that is honestly what I enjoy so much about cooking: the fun. At home I totally lean in to more of a casual, fun experience of a shared meal. In this book I have included not just my favourite baked goods, but also many dishes I created after visiting different countries. You'll see dishes from France and Spain, Mexico, and also Asian influences from Indonesia, Malaysia and Vietnam. I have crammed in as many flavours and as much fun as I can!

I often get asked why I love to cook. It's a combination of the process and the enjoyment it gives others when they taste what I've made. I feel most at peace when I cook, and I love to see the effect my food has on the people I love. Food brings everyone together, creates conversations and puts a smile on their face. I hope this book brings a smile to yours!

Breakfasts

There's nothing like starting your day off right with some good, delicious food. For me, breakfast should be something delicious but also achievable – nothing too complicated, just fun and yum. The Sunday morning big breakfast cook-up is a tradition in my family – why not make it yours?

Super-Simple Banana Pancakes

Total prep time	Total cook time	Serves	Difficulty
10 minutes	5 minutes	2	★☆☆

When I auditioned for *Junior MasterChef Australia* in 2010, we were asked to create a pancake dish with a twist. I chose to make banana pikelets, and I have been making banana pancakes ever since. This recipe is simple and delicious.

- 1 free-range egg
- 1 overripe banana
- ⅓ cup (50g) self-raising flour, sifted
- 1 teaspoon honey
- 1 teaspoon cinnamon sugar, plus extra to serve
- 1 tablespoon vegetable oil
- 2 bananas, sliced, to serve
- honey, extra to serve

In a bowl, combine the egg, banana, flour, 1 teaspoon honey and cinnamon sugar, and use a wooden spoon to mix until combined.

Heat a large fry pan over medium–low heat and add the vegetable oil. Carefully spoon the batter into the pan to form four even pancakes. Depending on the size of the pan, you might need to cook these in batches. Top each pancake with 4 slices of banana. Cook for 2–3 minutes and then flip and cook for a further 2–3 minutes or until golden brown. Remove from the heat and stack on a plate, then add a few extra banana slices and a pinch of cinnamon sugar and drizzle honey over the top to serve.

Be careful not to over-mix the pancake batter – we don't want any gluten to form, because this will make the pancakes tough and dry.

Breakfast Burrito

Total prep time	Total cook time	Makes	Difficulty
20 minutes	15 minutes	1	★★★

Big breakfast cook-ups with family and friends are one of my favourite times in the kitchen; the smell of freshly cooked bacon and eggs always makes waking up that little bit easier. This burrito is quick and fun to make, and most importantly, it's super delicious.

1 roma tomato, finely chopped

½ onion, peeled and finely chopped

½ bunch coriander, leaves picked and finely chopped

2 free-range eggs

2 tablespoons full-cream milk

2 rashers streaky bacon, cut into 2-centimetre strips

1 frozen hash brown (store bought)

1 large flour tortilla (store bought)

2 slices Monterey Jack cheese

1 tablespoon olive oil

1 tablespoon chipotle sauce (store bought)

1 tablespoon pickled jalapeños, finely chopped

¼ avocado, seeded and finely chopped

sea salt and freshly ground black pepper, to taste

Mix the tomato, onion and coriander in a bowl. Set this salsa aside while you prepare the rest of the burrito.

In a small bowl, combine the eggs and milk. Use a whisk or a fork to vigorously mix until combined. Set aside with the salsa.

Place a fry pan over low heat and add the bacon. Fry until crispy, then remove the bacon from the pan and set it aside. In the same pan, fry the hash brown in the bacon fat on both sides until crispy, then remove it from the pan and set it aside.

In the same pan over low heat, add the olive oil and then the egg mixture, and cook for 30 seconds, then add the flour tortilla to the top so it 'sticks' to the egg mixture. Carefully flip to toast the other side of the tortilla, then remove it from the pan and set it aside on a serving plate.

Working quickly so the tortilla doesn't go cold, add the crispy bacon back to the pan and top with the cheese. Allow the cheese to melt to create a bacon-cheese 'patty'.

To assemble the burrito, add the bacon 'patty' to the warmed tortilla, spread a layer of chipotle sauce, then top with the hash brown, the salsa, jalapeños and avocado, and season with salt and pepper. Once you have all the fillings in place, carefully fold the tortilla into a burrito – and enjoy!

Ultimate French Toast

Total prep time	Total cook time	Serves	Difficulty
30 minutes	10 minutes	4	★★☆

French toast always feels so decadent. It's a treat, let's be honest, so why not go all out?

8 rashers streaky bacon

¼ cup (60ml) maple syrup

½ cup (125ml) thickened cream

1 tablespoon caster sugar

1 teaspoon vanilla extract

2 free-range eggs

¼ cup full-cream milk

¼ cup cream

½ teaspoon ground cinnamon

2 tablespoons vegetable oil

4 thick slices brioche bread (store bought)

To serve

½ punnet blueberries

1 punnet strawberries, thinly sliced lengthways

1 quantity of my homemade honeycomb (see page 102)

watercress leaves

maple syrup

icing sugar, sifted

Preheat the oven to 200°C.

Line a baking tray with baking paper and lay out the bacon. Drizzle over the maple syrup and spread evenly with a pastry brush. Top with another piece of baking paper and another baking tray. Bake for 20 minutes or until golden brown.

In the bowl of an electric mixer fitted with a whisk attachment, add the cream, caster sugar and vanilla, and whip until soft peaks form. Set aside to serve.

In a wide, shallow bowl, add the eggs, milk, cream and cinnamon, and whisk until combined.

Heat a large fry pan over medium–low heat and add the vegetable oil. Use tongs to dip the brioche slices one at a time in the egg mixture and then place in the pan. Cook for 2 minutes or until golden brown and then turn the bread and cook for 2 minutes on the other side.

Arrange the bread in the middle of the plate and then top with the blueberries, strawberries and maple bacon. Add a dollop of whipped cream, then sprinkle the crumbed honeycomb over the top. Garnish with watercress and then finish with a drizzle of maple syrup and a dusting of icing sugar.

Corn and Pea Fritters with Avocado Salsa

Total prep time	Total cook time	Serves	Difficulty
15 minutes	5 minutes	6	★★★

These fritters are quick, easy and – most importantly – delicious. You can enjoy them at any time of the day.

For the avocado salsa

2 roma tomatoes, finely chopped

½ red onion, peeled and finely chopped

1 avocado, seeded and finely chopped

1 tablespoon olive oil

½ bunch coriander, leaves picked and finely chopped

juice of 1 lime

sea salt and freshly ground black pepper, to taste

For the fritters

2½ cups (300g) frozen mixed peas and corn, cooked as per packet instructions

1 cup (150g) self-raising flour

1 free-range egg

½ cup (125ml) full-cream milk

½ onion, peeled and finely chopped

1 clove garlic, peeled and crushed

sea salt and freshly ground black pepper, to taste

¼ cup (60ml) vegetable oil

lime wedges, to serve

To make the avocado salsa

Combine all the salsa ingredients in a bowl and stir to combine, then set aside while you make the fritters.

To make the fritters

In a large bowl, combine the peas, corn, flour, egg, milk, onion, garlic and seasoning, and mix with a wooden spoon to combine.

Add the vegetable oil to a fry pan over medium heat, then carefully spoon 2 tablespoons of the mixture per fritter into the pan, taking care not to overcrowd the pan, and cook in batches for 2–3 minutes, then carefully flip the fritters and cook for a further 2–3 minutes or until crispy and golden brown. Remove from the pan and top with the avocado salsa, and serve with lime wedges.

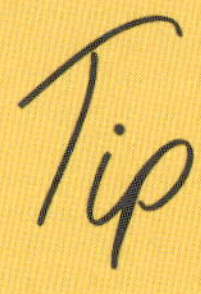

These fritters are a great breakfast, but they also make an awesome lunch or even served as an entree. They're super versatile! If you want to 'pimp' these, try adding a poached egg on top.

Nutella-Stuffed Pancakes

Total prep time 15 minutes, plus 1 hour freezing time for the Nutella | Total cook time 10 minutes | Serves 4 | Difficulty ★★★

My Nutella-stuffed pancakes make breakfast fun! There's nothing like seeing the surprise on someone's face when they cut into these pancakes to find the sweet filling. You will need to start this one early (at least 1 hour ahead) to ensure you set the Nutella nicely before you make the pancakes.

½ cup (140g) Nutella

2⅓ cups (350g) self-raising flour, sifted

¼ cup (55g) caster sugar

1¾ cups (440ml) full-cream milk

60 grams unsalted butter, melted

1 free-range egg

1 tablespoon vegetable oil

icing sugar, to serve

8 strawberries, finely chopped, to serve

Line a baking tray with baking paper. Using two spoons, form the Nutella into discs (around 8 centimetres in diameter) and place them on the tray, spacing them evenly. Gently flatten the discs to around 5 millimetres high, then place the tray in the freezer for at least 1 hour.

In a bowl, combine the flour, sugar, milk, butter and egg, and stir with a wooden spoon until just combined (there may still be flour lumps, but that's okay).

Remove the Nutella discs from the freezer.

Heat a large fry pan over medium–low heat and add the vegetable oil. Add 3 tablespoons of the pancake mixture to the pan to form one pancake, top with a frozen Nutella disc and then carefully pour a further 2 tablespoons of pancake mixture over the top, ensuring the mixture completely covers the Nutella. Cook for 3–4 minutes, then carefully flip the pancake mixture and cook for a further 3–4 minutes or until golden brown. Transfer the pancake to a serving plate while you repeat the process to make the remaining three pancakes. Top with a dusting of icing sugar and strawberries to serve.

Mains

Fun, tasty food doesn't get much better than this. Dinner is always a special time in my household – it's where we come together, share stories and debrief about what we got up to over the course of the day. This is where I like to be a bit more adventurous with my dishes.

Steak Frites

Total prep time	Total cook time	Serves	Difficulty
30 minutes	15 minutes	4	☆☆★

This dish holds a special place in my heart. I was such a fussy eater as a kid; I wouldn't try anything new. Finally, my dad convinced me to try my first steak – and boy, did I realise what I'd been missing. My first steak frites was at Thomas Keller's Bouchon Bistro in the Napa Valley in California. It was Bastille Day, and from that moment on, French fare was a part of my life.

For the triple-cooked chips

1 serve of The Best Chips Ever (page 162)

For the béarnaise sauce

4 tarragon sprigs, leaves picked

⅔ cup (160ml) white-wine vinegar

⅓ cup (80ml) white wine

8 whole black peppercorns

3 shallots, finely chopped

250 grams unsalted butter, room temperature, cut into cubes

3 free-range egg yolks

2 tablespoons finely chopped tarragon leaves, extra

sea salt and freshly ground black pepper, to taste

For the steak

4 x 200–300-gram pieces of your preferred cut of steak (mine is eye fillet or scotch fillet), room temperature

extra-virgin olive oil

sea salt and freshly ground black pepper, to season

1 handful chives, cut into 3-centimetre lengths

2 cloves garlic, peeled

100 grams unsalted butter

sea salt, to serve

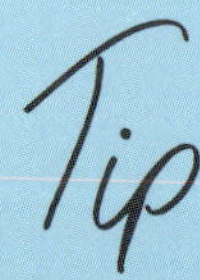

Don't rush the béarnaise sauce. Take your time adding the butter to the egg mixture, and make sure you don't stop whisking – otherwise you'll split your sauce.

To make the béarnaise sauce

In a saucepan over medium heat, combine the tarragon leaves, white-wine vinegar, wine, peppercorns and shallot. Bring to a boil, then reduce the heat and cook until the mixture has reduced by half. Set aside to cool slightly.

In a small saucepan, melt the butter over medium–high heat. Using a spoon, remove the milk solids that appear on the surface of the butter and discard. You should be left with a clear, gold liquid – this is clarified butter.

In a stainless-steel bowl, combine the egg yolks and finely chopped tarragon, and whisk together, then slowly pour in the warm reduced vinegar mixture while you keep whisking.

Place the stainless-steel bowl over a bain-marie (double boiler) on a low heat and whisk vigorously for 2–3 minutes or until the eggs thicken and turn pale. Keeping the bowl over the low heat, gradually add the butter, 1 tablespoon at a time, carefully continuing to whisk to ensure the mixture blends (emulsifies). Once all the butter is incorporated and the mixture is silky smooth, remove from the heat and set aside until ready to serve.

To make the steak

Coat both sides of the steaks with a generous amount of extra-virgin olive oil, salt and pepper.

Place a large fry pan over high heat and add enough extra-virgin oil to coat the bottom of the pan. When it is smoking hot, add the steaks and move them around the pan for the first few seconds of cooking so they don't stick. Reduce the heat to medium, then leave the beef to caramelise for 2–3 minutes, until a dark golden crust has formed. Turn the steaks over, then add the chives and garlic to the pan, followed by the butter. With a spoon, baste/drizzle the butter over the steaks for 2–3 minutes for a perfect medium–rare finish. (If you like your steak medium, cook for a further minute. For well done, cook for a further 2 minutes.)

Remove from the heat and allow to rest covered with foil on a warmed plate or baking tray for 5 minutes before serving.

To serve

Return your finished béarnaise sauce to the double boiler over low heat, continuously whisking for 1 minute to warm. Serve the steak with a sprinkle of salt and a drizzle of extra-virgin olive oil, accompanied by a generous handful of chips and the warmed barnaise sauce on the side.

Mushroom Risotto

Total prep time	Total cook time	Serves	Difficulty
15 minutes	35 minutes	4	★★☆

A good risotto can be so hard to nail, but that's what makes it so much more impressive when you do! And I promise, if you take your time, you'll get an awesome result.

9 cups (2.25 litres) chicken stock

2 tablespoons olive oil

3 shallots, finely chopped

90 grams dried shiitake mushrooms, soaked in boiling water and finely chopped

5 sprigs thyme, leaves picked

1½ cups (300g) arborio rice

sea salt and freshly ground black pepper, to taste

1¼ cups (100g) grated parmesan

1 knob unsalted butter

thyme leaves, to garnish

In a large saucepan, bring the chicken stock to a boil, then reduce the heat to low and keep on a simmer (just below a boil).

While the stock is heating up, place another saucepan over medium heat and add the olive oil. When it is hot, add the shallot and cook for 2–3 minutes or until tender, then add the mushroom and thyme, reduce the heat to low and cook for a further 5 minutes. Stir the rice into the mushroom and shallot mixture, and cook for 2 minutes or until the edges of the rice become translucent. (This step is incredibly important in the formation of a good risotto.)

Slowly add the hot chicken stock to the mushroom mixture one soup ladle at a time, while continuously stirring, adding more every time the stock is fully absorbed by the rice. Once the rice is al dente (cooked but still has a little crunch), season with salt and pepper, then remove from the heat and stir in the grated parmesan and butter. Garnish with the extra thyme leaves to serve.

Beef Rendang Bao

Total prep time	Total cook time	Makes	Difficulty
45 minutes, plus proving time for bao	4½ hours	15	☆☆☆

Bao is one of my favourite starters. The recipe is super versatile – you can fill it with everything from beef rendang, to fried chicken and even Mexican spiced pulled beef to make an Asian fusion taco. This recipe, especially the rendang, is quite long, so feel free to simplify it if you're in a rush – that could be anything from buying a pre-made filling for the bao to filling them with grilled chicken.

For the beef rendang

½ cup (75g) plain flour

1 teaspoon fine sea salt

800 grams braising beef (chuck or gravy), cut into large (approximately 3–4 centimetre) chunks (your butcher can do this for you)

¼ cup peanut oil (or vegetable oil)

1 large brown onion, peeled and finely chopped

3 cloves garlic, peeled and crushed

1 x 5-centimetre piece ginger, peeled and finely chopped

1 teaspoon ground turmeric

2 stalks lemongrass, white part only, finely chopped

2 red chillies, finely chopped

1 teaspoon tamarind paste

1 tablespoon ground coriander seeds

1 teaspoon freshly ground black pepper

1 cinnamon stick

2 kaffir lime leaves, finely sliced

½ cup (40g) toasted coconut

2 tablespoons palm sugar (or brown sugar)

sea salt, to season

3 cups (750ml) coconut milk

For the bao

3¼ cups (520g) bread flour

2 tablespoons caster sugar

7 grams dried yeast (or 15 g fresh yeast)

¼ cup (60ml) full-cream milk

2 tablespoons vegetable oil

1 teaspoon baking powder

1 cup (250ml) water

1 teaspoon fine sea salt

To serve

2 baby cucumbers, thinly sliced

2 bird's-eye chillies, thinly sliced

2 tablespoons crispy shallots

1 sprig coriander, leaves picked

To make the beef rendang

Preheat the oven to 140°C.

In a large bowl, combine the flour and salt, then add the beef and coat each piece with the mixture. Dust the remaining flour off and place the coated beef on a chopping board ready to be seared.

Place half the peanut oil in a large ovenproof casserole dish, and put the dish over medium heat. Working in batches, fry the meat until golden brown on all sides, transferring the cooked pieces to a plate while you fry the rest. Add the remaining oil to the dish, then add the onion, garlic, ginger and turmeric, and cook for 4–5 minutes or until the onion is soft. Add the lemongrass, chilli, tamarind paste, ground coriander, pepper, cinnamon, kaffir lime leaves, toasted coconut, palm sugar and salt to season. Mix together and cook for 1 minute. Add the coconut milk, then return the cooked beef to the casserole dish and give everything a good stir. Place a lid on the dish and transfer to the oven. Cook for 4 hours, giving the curry a stir every hour.

To make the bao

In the bowl of a stand mixer fitted with a dough hook, combine all the bao ingredients and mix for 10–15 minutes or until a 'gluten window' (see glossary) forms.

Grab another bowl about the same size, and spray it with canola oil. Transfer the dough to the bowl, cover with a tea towel and allow to rest and rise (prove) for 1 hour or until it has doubled in size.

To serve

Turn the dough onto a lightly floured surface and divide into 15 even pieces. Using a circular motion with the palm of your hand, gently roll each dough into a ball. Cover the dough balls with a clean cloth and allow them to rest for 10 minutes. Using a rolling pin, on a lightly floured surface roll each ball out to an oval 3–4 millimetres thick. Then fold each bao onto itself to create a half-moon shape.

Heat a large steamer over medium–high heat. Steam the buns for 8 minutes or until puffed up. While the buns are steaming, remove the rendang from the oven. Use two forks to carefully shred the beef (don't go crazy, we still want nice chunks of beef) while it is still in the sauce. Fill the steamed bao with a generous spoonful of the rendang, top with 2 slices of cucumber and sliced chilli, crispy shallots and coriander.

One-Pan Gnocchi

Total prep time	Total cook time	Serves	Difficulty
30 minutes	15 minutes	4	☆☆★

Gnocchi transforms the humble spud into amazingly light and fluffy pillows of joy. My recipe is a one-pan style where the gnocchi are cooked in the sauce, giving them even more flavour.

For the gnocchi

1 kilogram (7–8 medium) potatoes

3 teaspoons sea salt

1 free-range egg

1⅔ cups (250g) plain flour

For the sauce

6 rashers streaky bacon, finely chopped

1 tablespoon extra-virgin olive oil

1 onion, peeled and finely chopped

1 clove garlic, peeled and crushed

1 chicken breast, finely chopped

½ cup (125ml) chicken stock

½ cup (125ml) thickened cream

sea salt and freshly ground black pepper, to taste

½ cup (40g) grated parmesan

½ cup (40g) grated mozzarella

1 large handful spinach leaves

grated parmesan, extra, to serve

Special equipment

Potato ricer

To make the gnocchi

Place the potatoes (unpeeled) in a large saucepan and add enough cold water to cover the potatoes, then add half of the sea salt. Place the saucepan over high heat and bring the water to a boil, then reduce the heat to medium, and cook for 10–15 minutes or until you can just poke a fork through the potatoes.

Remove the potatoes from the water and leave them to cool, then peel them. Pass the potatoes through a potato ricer or push through a fine sieve into a large bowl. Add the egg, flour and remaining salt, and stir with a wooden spoon until combined.

Divide the gnocchi dough into 4 equal portions. Using your hands, form 1 portion into a log 2 centimetres in diameter and 30 centimetres long, and place it on a clean, dry surface. Use a lightly floured knife to cut the log into 2-centimetre pieces. Repeat with the remaining dough portions.

Lightly flour your hands, and roll each piece of dough into a ball. Use your thumb to roll each ball over a floured fork. Place your gnocchi on a lightly floured tray while you prepare the sauce.

To make the sauce

Heat a fry pan over medium heat. Add half the bacon, and cook until crispy, then remove from the pan and set aside. In the same pan, add the extra-virgin olive oil and then the onion and garlic, and cook for 2 minutes. Add the remaining bacon and the chicken, and cook for 3–4 minutes minutes or until golden brown. Add the chicken stock, cream and the gnocchi, then reduce the heat to medium–low and cook for 3–5 minutes or until the sauce thickens and the gnocchi floats to the surface. Remove from the heat, season with salt and pepper, then add the cheeses and spinach and stir to combine. Top with the crispy bacon and grated parmesan to serve.

Mint and Honey Lamb Cutlets

Total prep time	Total cook time	Serves	Difficulty
20 minutes, plus marinating time	15 minutes	4	★★★

This quick and easy recipe is a go-to for weeknight meals in my family. The crispy, sweet layer on the outside of the cutlets makes them irresistible. If I have more time, I like to let the lamb soak in the marinade overnight.

For the marinade

¼ cup loosely packed mint leaves, finely chopped

¼ cup (60ml) boiling water

2 tablespoons white-wine vinegar

2 tablespoons caster sugar

⅓ cup (115g) honey

sea salt and freshly ground black pepper, to taste

For the lamb

12 frenched lamb cutlets

1 tablespoon olive oil

lemon wedges, to serve

In a large bowl, combine all the marinade ingredients and mix until combined. Allow the marinade to cool for 10 minutes, then place the lamb cutlets in the marinade, turning to coat them. Refrigerate for between 2 and 24 hours (the longer the better, to really let the flavour soak in). Remove the cutlets from the fridge 30 minutes prior to cooking.

Heat a large fry pan over high heat with the olive oil. Add the cutlets, and cook for 2 minutes, then carefully turn the cutlets and cook for a further 2 minutes on the other side; the outside should become crispy and caramelised. Remove the cutlets from the heat and allow them to rest for 5 minutes, then serve with the lemon wedges. They are amazing with my Crispy Smashed Potatoes (page 40).

Crispy Smashed Potatoes

Total prep time	Total cook time	Serves	Difficulty
15 minutes	50 minutes	4	★☆☆

This is the perfect crunchy-yet-soft side dish.

8 medium potatoes (King Edward, Desiree or Royal Blue varieties are best)

1 tablespoon sea salt

4 sprigs thyme, leaves picked

4 sprigs rosemary, leaves picked

sea salt and freshly ground black pepper, to taste

olive oil

Preheat the oven to 220°C. Line a baking tray with baking paper.

Peel and wash the potatoes, then place them in a large saucepan and add enough cold water to cover the potatoes. Add the tablespoon of sea salt to the water. Place the saucepan over high heat and bring the water to a boil, then reduce the heat to low and cook for 8–10 minutes or until you can just poke a fork through the potatoes. Drain the water.

Transfer the potatoes to the tray and use a potato masher to squish them. Top with the thyme, rosemary, a generous pinch of salt and pepper and finally a generous drizzle of oil. Bake for 30–40 minutes or until the potatoes are golden and crispy. Enjoy immediately.

Tip

This is one of my favourite side dishes. Depending on what I'm serving the potatoes with, I might add some different herbs or spices such as paprika or oregano, so feel free to play around and add any of your favourites!

Beef and Lamb Dumplings

Total prep time	Total cook time	Makes around	Difficulty
30 minutes	10 minutes	30	☆☆★

Doesn't everyone love dumplings? These bad boys are a favourite when I entertain family and friends.

- 6 dried shiitake mushrooms
- 2 cups Chinese cabbage, finely chopped
- 1 teaspoon sea salt
- 125 grams beef mince
- 125 grams lamb mince
- ½ bunch chives, finely chopped
- 1 tablespoon soy sauce
- 2 teaspoons rice-wine vinegar
- 1 garlic clove, peeled and crushed
- 1 x 2-centimetre piece ginger, peeled and grated
- 30 round dumpling wrappers (store bought)
- vegetable oil
- ½ cup (125ml) water
- finely sliced chives, to serve
- soy sauce, to dip
- zhenjiang vinegar, to dip
- chilli oil, to dip

Place the shiitake mushrooms in a bowl and cover with boiling water, then allow to rest for 15 minutes. Squeeze out the excess water and finely chop the mushrooms.

Place the cabbage in a bowl with the salt and toss to combine, then set aside for 15 minutes. Squeeze out the excess liquid.

In a large bowl, place the beef, lamb, finely chopped chives, soy sauce, rice-wine vinegar, garlic and ginger, and mix to combine.

Dip your finger in water and moisten the outer edge of half a dumpling wrapper (in a semi-circle). Place 1 tablespoon of filling in the middle. Start by folding the dumpling in half and pinching the wrapper edges together at the meeting point at the top. Then, on each side of the dumpling, make two pleats starting with the inside (closest to the middle). Then make another two pleats on the outer corners of the dumpling, again towards the middle. Make sure that all seams are sealed.

Heat 1 tablespoon vegetable oil in a large pan over medium heat. Working in batches, add the dumplings in a single layer and cook for 30 seconds or until the bottoms begin to brown. Add the water, cover with a lid and cook the dumplings for 3 minutes, then uncover and cook for a further 2 minutes or until the liquid has evaporated and the bottoms are crisp and golden brown. Repeat with the remaining dumplings, adding more vegetable oil as needed. Serve immediately scattered with the finely sliced chives and bowls of soy sauce, zhenjiang vinegar and chilli oil.

Confit Duck with Red Cabbage, Chickpeas and Jus

Total prep time	Total cook time	Serves	Difficulty
1 hour, plus brine time	4½ hours	4	★★★

This is one of my favourite meals to cook for a special occasion. It's certainly not a cheap dish to make but I can assure you, your loved ones will thoroughly enjoy it.

For the confit duck

2½ cups (500g) rock salt

zest of 1 orange

zest of 1 lemon

1 x 5-centimetre piece ginger, peeled and grated

4 star anise

2 cloves garlic, peeled and crushed

4 duck marylands

1 tablespoon Chinese five-spice powder

3 cups (750g) duck fat, melted

For the pickled cabbage

3 cups (1kg) sliced red cabbage

¼ cup (55g) caster sugar

1 teaspoon salt

1 cup (250ml) rice-wine vinegar (or apple-cider vinegar)

For the crispy chickpeas

1 x 400-gram can chickpeas, drained and washed

olive oil, to drizzle

sea salt and freshly ground black pepper

For the jus

2 tablespoons olive oil

4 shallots, finely chopped

3 teaspoons honey

½ teaspoon Chinese five-spice powder

1½ cups (350ml) port

1 tablespoon red-wine vinegar

2 cups (500ml) chicken stock

2 cups (500ml) beef stock

sea salt and freshly ground black pepper, to season

PTO for the cooking steps

Tip

Confit: this is a classic method of preserving meat, from before the days of refrigeration. The process gives meat a great texture and flavour. I promise my confit duck legs are worth the wait!

To make the confit duck

The day prior

In a baking dish, combine the rock salt, orange and lemon zest, ginger, star anise and garlic. Place the duck skin-side down on top of the salt mixture, and use your hands to rub the flesh with the five-spice powder. Refrigerate for at least 5 hours or ideally overnight.

The day of

Preheat the oven to 120°C.

Place the duck fat in a deep roasting pan and transfer to the oven for 10 minutes to warm and melt, then remove the roasting pan from the oven but keep the oven on. Remove the duck from the salt coating and brush off any excess salt, then place the duck in the warmed fat, taking care to completely submerge the duck in the fat. Bake for 3–4 hours or until the meat is tender and almost falling off the bone. Remove the duck from the oven and scoop out around 1 cup of the duck fat. (You can keep the remaining duck fat for roasting vegetables. It will be fine sealed in the fridge for up to 2 months.)

To make the pickled cabbage

In a saucepan, combine the cabbage, caster sugar, salt and rice-wine vinegar. Place the saucepan over low heat and stir until it comes to a boil. Remove from the heat and allow to cool completely.

To make the crispy chickpeas

Preheat the oven to 200°C. Line a baking tray with baking paper.

Scatter the chickpeas across the baking tray, drizzle with olive oil and scatter with salt and pepper. Roast for 20–30 minutes or until crispy. Remove from the oven and allow to cool completely.

To make the jus

In a saucepan, combine the olive oil, shallot, honey and five-spice powder. Place the saucepan over medium heat and cook for 6–8 minutes or until the mixture has caramelised and is sticky. Add the port, red-wine vinegar and stock, and bring to a boil, then reduce the heat to low and cook for 30 minutes or until the liquid has reduced by half. Taste for seasoning, add salt and pepper if you feel it needs it, then carefully pour through a fine sieve, to capture any solids. Discard the solids. Keep the jus warm until serving.

To serve

Place a large fry pan over high heat and, working in batches, add around 2 tablespoons of the reserved duck fat at a time and fry the duck skin-side down until it is crispy and warmed through. Serve the confit duck with the jus on a bed of pickled cabbage, topped with the crispy chickpeas.

Perfect Mashed Potato

Total prep time	Total cook time	Serves	Difficulty
15 minutes	30 minutes	4	☆☆★

I hate lumpy mashed potato so much that I used to puree my mash to ensure it was completely smooth. Nowadays I've realised there's no need to puree your mash if it's made properly. Here's how.

1 kilogram Dutch Cream potatoes, peeled and washed

1 teaspoon salt

¾ cup (185ml) full-cream milk

200 grams unsalted butter, softened, cut into cubes

salt, to taste

finely chopped parsley, to serve

finely chopped chives, to serve

1 knob unsalted butter, to serve

Special equipment

Potato ricer

Place the potatoes in a large saucepan with enough water to cover the potatoes, and the teaspoon of salt. Place the saucepan over a medium–low heat and cook for 15–25 minutes or until you can just poke a fork through the potatoes. Drain the water but keep the saucepan handy – you will need it again.

Pass the potatoes through the potato ricer, then return them to the saucepan. (If you don't have a potato ricer, you can push the potatoes through a sieve using the back of a spoon.) Place the saucepan over a low heat and stir with a wooden spoon for 2–3 minutes.

Meanwhile, place the milk in a small saucepan and set it over a low heat. Bring it to a boil, then remove from the heat. Add the butter to the potato and then, while you are mixing the potato, slowly pour in the hot milk. Stir for 4 minutes and season to taste. Transfer to a serving bowl and top with the parsley, chives and butter.

Steak Quesadillas

Total prep time	Total cook time	Serves	Difficulty
30 minutes	15 minutes	4	☆☆★

Quesadillas are my favourite Mexican dish. Here with my steak quesadillas I have taken a quick and simple approach to a timeless classic. You'll find these on my dinner table at least once a week.

2 x 200–300-gram pieces of your preferred cut of steak (mine is eye fillet or scotch fillet), room temperature

olive oil

2 tablespoons Mexican seasoning powder (store bought)

4 flour tortillas (store bought)

2 tablespoons caramelised onion (store bought)

8 slices pickled jalapeños

8 slices Monterey Jack cheese (or half mozzarella and half tasty)

2 tablespoons Sriracha Kewpie mayonnaise (you can find this in most supermarkets)

sea salt and freshly ground black pepper, to taste

parmesan, grated, to garnish

chopped coriander leaves, to garnish

Coat both sides of the steak with olive oil and the Mexican seasoning powder. Allow to marinate for 30 minutes.

Place a fry pan over high heat and add enough olive oil to coat the bottom of the pan. When it is smoking hot, add the steaks and move them around the pan for the first few seconds of cooking so they don't stick. Reduce the heat to medium, then leave the beef to caramelise for 2–3 minutes, until a dark-golden crust has formed. Turn the steak and cook for a further 3 minutes for a perfect medium–rare finish. (If you like your steak medium, cook for a further minute. For well done, cook for a further 2 minutes.) Remove from the heat and allow to rest for 5 minutes.

Top one half of each tortilla with the steak, then add a quarter of the caramelised onion, jalapeños, cheese and mayonnaise, and season with salt and pepper. Fold the other half of the tortilla over the top. Grill the tortilla in a clean pan with olive oil for 2 minutes on each side. Top with the parmesan and coriander to serve.

Slow-Cooked Lamb Lasagna

Total prep time	Total cook time	Serves	Difficulty
40 minutes	2½ hours	6	☆☆★

Lasagna is one of my favorite meals that Mum made as I was growing up. There's something so comforting about it. Mum's lasagna was completely different to my version, but there's always room for both! My take on lasagna combines lovely slow-cooked lamb shoulder in a rich ragu with homemade béchamel sauce and pasta – it doesn't get much better than that.

For the lamb ragu

¼ cup (60ml) olive oil

1.2-kilogram boneless lamb shoulder, cut into bite-sized pieces (your butcher can do this for you)

4 cloves garlic, peeled and crushed

1 onion, peeled and finely chopped

3 carrots, peeled and finely chopped

3 sticks celery, finely chopped

2 x 400-gram cans crushed tomatoes

⅓ cup (100g) tomato paste

2 cups (500ml) beef stock

4 sprigs thyme, leaves picked

3 dried bay leaves

sea salt and freshly ground black pepper, to season

For the béchamel sauce

60 grams unsalted butter

⅓ cup (50g) plain flour

4½ cups (1.125L) full-cream milk

½ cup (50g) grated Monterey Jack cheese

½ cup (50g) grated cheddar

½ cup (40g) grated parmesan

½ cup (50g) grated mozzarella

pinch of ground nutmeg

pinch of sea salt and freshly ground black pepper

For the lasagna

350 grams fresh lasagna sheets (store bought)

2 cups (200g) grated mozzarella

PTO for the cooking steps

Tip

Please make sure you follow my advice and place the ragu in the baking tray first so that the first layer of pasta doesn't dry out and stick to the pan. And, take your time to layer and assemble this beauty.

To make the lamb ragu

Preheat the oven to 140°C.

Heat 2 tablespoons of olive oil in a large oven-proof casserole dish over high heat, then add the lamb and cook for 2–3 minutes or until it has browned. Remove the lamb from the dish and set it aside. In the same dish, heat the remaining oil over high heat, then add the garlic and onion and cook for 2 minutes. Add the carrot and celery and cook for a further 5 minutes or until the vegetables are soft.

Return the lamb to the pan and add the tomato, tomato paste, beef stock, thyme and bay leaves, and season with salt and pepper. Stir to combine the mixture, then cover with a lid and transfer to the oven. Bake for 2 hours, but over that time check and stir it every 30 minutes to make sure everything is mixing together nicely. It will smell amazing!

Once the ragu is cooked, remove it from the oven. Use two forks to carefully shred the lamb while it is still in the sauce. Taste it, and if it needs more seasoning, add some salt and pepper.

To make the béchamel sauce

Have all your ingredients measured and ready, because you need to make the sauce quickly. In a medium saucepan over low heat, melt the butter, then add the flour and cook, stirring constantly, for 1–2 minutes. Remove from the heat, then slowly add the milk while stirring vigorously. Return the saucepan to a low heat and stir with a wooden spoon for 8–10 minutes or until the mixture has thickened and just comes to a boil. Remove from the heat and stir in the cheeses, nutmeg, salt and pepper. Set aside while you assemble the lasagna.

To assemble

Preheat the oven to 180°C. Grease a 20 x 30 centimetre baking dish.

Spoon 1 cup of the ragu into the base of the baking dish, then cover with lasagna sheets. Spread a thick layer of ragu over the lasagna sheets, then spread a thin layer each of bechamel and mozzarella over the ragu. Repeat this layering process until the top of baking dish is reached, ensuring your top layer is cheese.

Bake for 30–35 minutes or until the top is golden and bubbling.

Nasi Goreng

Total prep time	Total cook time	Serves	Difficulty
15 minutes	10 minutes	2	★☆☆

Whenever I travelled through Asia as a kid, especially Indonesia and Malaysia, nasi goreng was a staple, and often I would get frustrated upon returning home when I couldn't find a fried rice that compared. So, what did I do? I got busy in the kitchen to create my own version.

- 2½ tablespoons peanut oil (or vegetable oil)
- 1 chicken breast, cut into bite-sized pieces
- 1 shallot, finely chopped
- 20 grams dried shiitake mushroom, soaked in boiling water and finely chopped
- ½ carrot, peeled and finely chopped
- 2 kaffir lime leaves, thinly sliced
- 1 bird's-eye chilli, finely chopped
- ½ teaspoon terasi (Indonesian shrimp paste, optional)
- 1 x 250-gram packet of microwave jasmine rice, cooked according to instructions
- ⅓ cup (50g) frozen peas
- 2 tablespoons kecap manis
- 1 free-range egg
- crispy shalllots, to serve
- coriander leaves, to serve

Heat a wok over high heat, then add 1 tablespoon peanut oil and the chicken breast. Cook for 2–3 minutes or until the meat just starts to turn brown. Remove from the wok and set aside.

Add another 1 tablespoon peanut oil, then the shallot, mushroom, carrot, lime leaves, chilli and terasi (if using). Cook for 2–3 minutes or until it starts to smell amazing. Return the chicken to the wok along with the rice, and stir to combine. Add the peas and kecap manis, and stir-fry until everything is combined.

Add the remaining peanut oil to coat a separate pan, then fry the egg sunny-side up – the white should be firm and the yolk still a little runny.

Serve up the rice, and top with the egg. Garnish with crispy shallots and coriander leaves.

Pesto Salami Fettuccine

Total prep time	Total cook time	Serves	Difficulty
15 minutes	15 minutes	4	★☆☆

This quick and easy pasta is a go-to weeknight meal for me.

- 2 tablespoons extra-virgin olive oil
- 2 cloves garlic, peeled and crushed
- 1 onion, peeled and finely chopped
- 100 grams hot salami slices, halved
- 1 punnet sweet cherry tomatoes, halved
- 2 teaspoons sea salt
- 450 grams fresh fettuccine (or 250g if you use dry pasta)
- ½ cup (100g) basil pesto
- ¼ cup spinach leaves
- freshly grated parmesan, to serve

In a fry pan over medium heat, add the extra-virgin olive oil, garlic and onion, and cook, stirring, for 4–5 minutes or until the onion is soft and it all smells delicious. Add the salami slices and cherry tomatoes, and cook until the salami turns crispy and the tomatoes blister. Remove from the heat but keep the mixture in the fry pan.

Add 1 litre of water to a large saucepan and place over high heat. Bring the water to a boil and add the salt. Add the pasta, and cook as per the packet instructions – minus 1 minute. Remove from the heat and drain the pasta, saving ⅓ cup of the pasta water. Add the cooked pasta to the onion mixture, along with the pesto, spinach and the reserved pasta water. Place the pan over high heat and toss to combine everything. Serve immediately topped with parmesan.

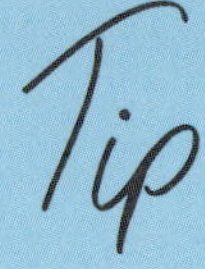

If you've got some extra time, this dish works really well with my homemade tagliatelle (page 60).

Chicken, Chilli and Lemongrass Stir-Fry

Total prep time	Total cook time	Serves	Difficulty
20 minutes	20 minutes	4	☆☆★

This is one of my favourite Vietnamese dishes. Once I moved on from chicken nuggets as a kid (you must check out my take on this old favourite, page 138), this stir-fry became my regular choice at our local Vietnamese restaurant.

2 cups (400g) jasmine rice, rinsed in cold water

4 cups (1L) coconut water

2 tablespoons peanut oil (or vegetable oil)

3 chicken breasts or thighs, cut into small strips

2 bird's-eye chillies, finely sliced (seeds removed if you don't like heat)

1 lemongrass stalk, white part only, finely sliced

1 onion, peeled and finely chopped

2 cloves garlic, peeled and crushed

1 bunch Chinese broccoli, cut into pieces

2 teaspoons palm sugar

1 tablespoon fish sauce

⅓ cup (60ml) oyster sauce

½ cup (125ml) coconut cream

coriander leaves, to serve

lime wedges, to serve

extra sliced chilli, to serve

black sesame seeds, to garnish (optional)

Add the rice and coconut water to a medium saucepan, and bring to a boil. Allow the rice to boil for 4–5 minutes, then stir and reduce the heat to low. Cover and leave for 8 minutes – do *not* lift the lid!

Heat a wok over high heat and add the oil. Add the chicken, and stir-fry for 2 minutes or until browned, then remove from the wok and set aside. Add the chilli, lemongrass, onion, garlic and Chinese broccoli to the wok, and stir-fry for 2 minutes or until it starts to smell delicious. Return the chicken to the wok and stir to combine, then add the palm sugar, fish sauce, oyster sauce and coconut cream, and bring to a boil. Serve immediately garnished with the coriander leaves, lime and chilli, with the coconut rice (sprinkled with black sesame seeds, if you like).

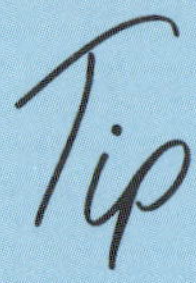

A good wok makes a big difference in this recipe. Don't be afraid to (carefully) crank up the heat and get it smoking hot!

Tagliatelle with Beef Ragu

Total prep time	Total cook time	Serves	Difficulty
45 minutes	2½ hours	4	★★★

I love a good pasta dish – but it needs to be done right. This recipe is my take on spag bol, except ten times better! Even though this recipe requires a few hours to cook, I promise you it's worth it, and if you make your own pasta it'll be even better. But if you want to save some time, don't sweat – you can always grab store-bought tagliatelle.

For the beef ragu

¼ cup (60ml) olive oil

1.2 kilograms chuck steak, cut into 6-centimetre cubes (your butcher can do this for you)

4 cloves garlic, peeled and crushed

1 onion, peeled and finely chopped

3 carrots, peeled and finely chopped

3 sticks celery, finely chopped

2 x 400-gram cans crushed tomatoes

¼ cup (70g) tomato paste

2 cups (500ml) beef stock

4 sprigs thyme, leaves picked

3 dried bay leaves

sea salt and freshly ground black pepper, to taste

basil leaves, to serve

shaved parmesan, to serve

For the tagliatelle

2 cups (300g) 00 flour

3 large free-range eggs

Special equipment

Pasta machine

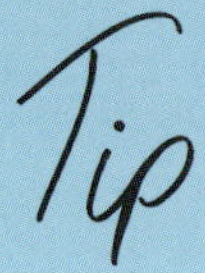

When browning off the chuck steak, ensure you get a golden-brown crust on the meat. Don't rush this process – it's the base of achieving a great flavour. If you want to skip a step, you can buy ready-made pasta to serve with my beautiful ragu.

To make the beef ragu

Add the olive oil to a large fry pan over high heat. Add the beef and cook for 2–3 minutes or until brown on all sides, then remove from the pan and set aside. Add the garlic and onion to the same pan, and cook for 2 minutes, then add the carrot and celery, and cook for a further 5 minutes or until the vegetables are soft. Return the meat to the pan and add the crushed tomato, tomato paste, stock, thyme, bay leaves, salt and pepper. Cover the pan with a lid, and cook on low heat for 2 hours, stirring occasionally.

To make the tagliatelle

Place three-quarters of the flour into a mound on a clean, dry bench and use your hands to make a well in the centre. Crack the eggs into this well, use a fork to lightly beat the eggs, then mix in the flour a little at a time. If the dough is too sticky to handle, add the remaining flour until it becomes workable. With your hands, bring the mixture together and form it into a nice ball of dough, then keep kneading it for 10 minutes or until the dough is smooth and elastic. Cover your dough with a tea towel and rest it in the fridge for 30 minutes.

Divide the dough into 4 equal pieces, then use a pasta machine to roll it out to a sheet 3-millimetres thick. Dust each sheet with flour, then fold it up, starting at one end. Use a knife to cut the pasta into 1-centimetre strips to create the tagliatelle. Unravel the cut tagliatelle strips and twirl into 'nests'. Dust generously with flour to stop the pasta from sticking together.

To serve

Place a large pot of salted water over high heat and bring it to a boil. Add your tagliatelle and cook for 3–5 minutes or until al dente – just soft enough to eat but still a little firm. Use two forks to carefully shred the beef (don't over-do it, we still want nice chunks of beef) while it is still in the sauce. Drain the tagliatelle and stir through the ragu (remove the bay leaves just before you serve), then top with basil and parmesan to serve.

Slow-Roasted Lamb Shoulder

Total prep time	Total cook time	Serves	Difficulty
30 minutes	5 hours	4	★★★

Once you try my slow-roasted lamb shoulder, you'll never be able to go back to the plain old Sunday roast again. Don't be scared by the long cook time, it honestly is a set-and-forget recipe, making it perfect for a lazy weekend in.

For the lamb:

1 tablespoon olive oil

1 x 1.8-kilogram lamb shoulder, bone in (your butcher can help you choose the right size depending on how many people you plan to feed)

1 cup (250ml) water

2 tablespoons olive oil, extra

1 tablespoon sea salt flakes

1 teaspoon freshly ground black pepper

1 tablespoon finely chopped rosemary leaves

1 tablespoon finely chopped thyme leaves

2 bulbs garlic, cut in half

2 onions, cut in half

For the gravy

1 tablespoon plain flour

1½ cups (375ml) chicken stock

To make the lamb

Preheat the oven to 180°C.

In a fry pan over high heat, add 1 tablespoon olive oil and the lamb shoulder, and cook on both sides until golden brown.

Add the water to the base of a large roasting pan, then grab a wire rack that fits over the top. Place the lamb on the rack and top with the remaining olive oil, salt, pepper, rosemary and thyme, then rub the toppings all in to combine and really soak into the meat.

Reduce the oven temperature to 140°C, and roast the lamb for 2 hours. Remove the lamb from the oven and cover it with foil, then add the garlic and onion to the pan and return it to the oven to roast for a further 3 hours.

Remove the lamb from the oven and, with it still wrapped in foil, allow it to rest for 10 minutes while you make the gravy. When you have made the gravy and are ready to serve, unwrap the lamb from the foil and carve it – the meat should shred off the bone.

To make the gravy

While the lamb is resting, make the gravy. Tip the excess fat from the roasting pan into a bowl and set aside. Place the roasting pan over medium heat, then add the flour and 1 tablespoon of the reserved fat. Using a wooden spoon, stir well to pick up the sediment from the pan and cook for 2 minutes. Add the stock and continue to cook, stirring, for a further 3 minutes or until thickened, then strain through a sieve into a jug and serve with the lamb.

This is great served with my Perfect Roast Potatoes (see page 66).

Perfect Roast Potatoes

Total prep time	Total cook time	Serves	Difficulty
15 minutes	55 minutes	4	★☆☆

Growing up, I used to hate potatoes, especially roast potatoes. Looking back now I'm not sure why, because I always loved French fries! The recipe for my perfect roast potatoes has come after years and years of practice with different types of potatoes, in different types of oil with different types of seasonings. But I'm fairly confident in saying I've now nailed it. Here's how.

- 1 kilogram kipfler potatoes (King Edward potatoes also work well)
- sea salt flakes
- ½ cup (125ml) peanut oil (peanut oil has a higher smoking point than most oils, but if you have a nut allergy you can use grapeseed or sunflower oil instead)
- 1 teaspoon celery salt
- 1 teaspoon finely chopped rosemary leaves
- 1 teaspoon finely chopped thyme leaves
- 1 teaspoon freshly ground black pepper

Preheat the oven to 220°C. Line a large baking tray with baking paper.

Peel and wash the potatoes thoroughly (if you are using kipfler potatoes, the majority can be left whole; if you are using regular potatoes, chop them into bite-sized pieces). Place the potatoes in a large saucepan and add enough cold water to cover the potatoes. Add 1 teaspoon of the salt to the water. Place the saucepan over high heat and bring the water to a boil; once boiling, reduce the heat to low and cook for 8–10 minutes or until you can just poke a fork through the potatoes. Drain the water.

Drizzle half the oil over the baking paper. Add the potatoes, making sure not to overcrowd the tray (there should be at least 2–3 centimetres between each potato; use a second tray if you need to). Sprinkle over the celery salt, rosemary, thyme, 1 teaspoon salt and the pepper, and top with the remaining oil.

Bake the potatoes for 45 minutes or until they are golden brown and crispy, turning halfway and adding more oil if necessary. Remove from the oven and serve immediately – it's important to note that the longer you leave these potatoes once they come out of the oven the less crispy they will be, so I suggest you enjoy them straightaway.

Philly Cheesesteak Mac-and-Cheese

Total prep time	Total cook time	Serves	Difficulty
20 minutes	1 hour	4	★☆☆

A traditional cheesesteak is a sandwich that originated in Philadelphia. It is made from thinly sliced steak and melted cheese in a long roll. I've taken inspiration from this American classic and turned it into one of the most comforting comfort-food dishes you could ever dream of!

1 tablespoon extra-virgin olive oil

1 x 300-grams sirloin steak, thinly sliced

extra-virgin olive oil, extra

2 onions, peeled and sliced

2 tablespoons brown sugar

2 teaspoons sea salt

1 cup (250g) macaroni pasta

⅓ cup (40g) panko breadcrumbs

30 grams unsalted butter, melted

⅓ cup (50g) plain flour

60 grams unsalted butter, extra

3 cups (750ml) full-cream milk

2 cups (200g) grated cheese of your choice (mozzarella, Monterey Jack or any other melting cheese)

sea salt and freshly ground black pepper, to taste

finely chopped parsley, to garnish

Heat the extra-virgin olive oil in a large fry pan over high heat, then add the sliced steak and cook for 3–4 minutes or until it has browned and started to caramelise. Remove from the pan and set aside.

In the same fry pan, heat some extra-virgin olive oil over low heat, then add the onion, and cook for 10 minutes or until tender. Add the brown sugar, and cook for a further 30 minutes, stirring every few minutes or until the mixture is deeply caramelised. Remove from the pan and set aside with the steak.

Preheat the oven to 180°C. Grease a deep, 18 x 30-centimetre baking dish.

Add 1 litre of water to a large saucepan and place over high heat. Bring the water to a boil and add the 2 teaspoons sea salt, then add the macaroni and cook as per the packet instructions – minus 1 minute. Remove from the heat and drain the pasta.

In a bowl, combine the breadcrumbs and the melted butter, and set aside.

In the same fry pan as the onion, add the flour and remaining butter, and stir for 2 minutes, to create a roux, then add the milk and stir briskly until the mixture is smooth.

Add the steak, onion and macaroni, and stir to combine. Add the cheese, then season with salt and pepper, and mix to combine. Transfer the mixture to your baking dish, top with the panko topping and bake for 30 minutes or until golden and caramelised. Remove from the oven and garnish with parsley to serve.

Massaman Curry with Roti Canai

Total prep time
1 hour, plus mininum 5 hours' resting time for the roti canai and marinating time for the beef

Total cook time
5 hours

Serves
4

Difficulty
☆☆☆

This is one of my favourite curries – there's something about the mix of lightness and richness that works together so well. It goes perfectly with my roti canai to soak up all that leftover sauce. It's far from quick and easy, but I promise it's worth it.

For the curry

1 cup (250ml) kecap manis

1 kilogram chuck steak, cut into 6-centimetre cubes (your butcher can do this for you)

3 tablespoons peanut oil (or vegetable oil)

2 cups (500ml) coconut cream

sea salt

2 shallots, finely chopped

2 teaspoons palm sugar

1 teaspoon fish sauce

⅔ cup (100g) peanuts

sea salt and freshly ground black pepper, to season

3 medium potatoes, peeled and cut into 2.5-centimetre pieces

1 tablespoon peanuts, to serve

1 bird's-eye chilli, thinly sliced, to serve

1 bunch coriander, to serve

For the braising liquid

2 stalks lemongrass, white part only, finely chopped

3 knobs galangal, finely chopped

1 bird's-eye chilli, finely chopped

1 shallot, finely chopped

1½ cups (375ml) coconut cream

2 cups (500ml) water

¾ cup (190ml) chicken stock

¼ cup (60ml) fish sauce

⅔ cup (130g) palm sugar

For the spice paste

1 stalk lemongrass, white part only

5 dried red Asian chillies

4 shallots, peeled

4 cloves garlic, peeled

1 x 4-centimetre piece galangal, peeled

⅓ cup (80ml) water

½ teaspoon ground cloves

1 teaspoon ground cumin

¾ teaspoon ground coriander

½ teaspoon ground cardamom

For the roti canai

2¾ cups (415g) plain flour

½ cup (125ml) full-cream milk

⅔ cup (165ml) water

pinch of salt

pinch of sugar

50 grams unsalted butter, softened

peanut oil (or vegetable oil)

PTO for the cooking steps

To make the curry (part 1)

Place the kecap manis in a large bowl, and add the beef, turning to coat the meat, then refrigerate, covered, overnight.

The next day, remove the meat from the kecap manis and drain off any excess. Heat a fry pan over medium heat and add half the oil, then sauté the beef on all sides for 2–3 minutes or until golden brown. Set it aside while you make the braising liquid.

To make the braising liquid

Preheat the oven to 150°C.

Add the oil to a large ovenproof casserole dish over medium heat. Add the lemongrass, galangal, chilli and shallot and cook for 2–3 minutes or until you start to smell the amazing flavours. Add the coconut cream, water, stock, fish sauce and palm sugar, and increase the heat to high to bring it to a boil. Add the browned beef to the pot, cover with a tightly fitting lid and cook in the oven for 3½–4 hours or until the meat is very tender.

To make the spice paste

Place all the spice paste ingredients in a food processor and blitz on high speed for 1 minute or until a paste forms.

To make the curry (part 2)

In an ovenproof casserole dish over medium heat, combine 1 cup of the coconut cream, the remaining oil and a generous pinch of sea salt. Increase heat to high and bring the liquid to a boil. Add the spice paste and cook for 1 hour, stirring often. Add ¾ cup of the beef braising liquid, the remaining 1 cup coconut cream and the palm sugar, fish sauce and peanuts, then reduce the heat to low, and cook for 5–8 minutes. Taste the mixture and season with salt and pepper.

Add the potato and cook for 10 minutes. Add the beef and cook for a further 10 minutes to ensure the meat is warmed through. Garnish with the chilli, coriander and peanuts, and serve with the roti canai.

To make the roti canai

In the bowl of a stand mixer fitted with a dough hook, combine the flour, milk, water, salt and sugar, and mix on low speed for 10 minutes or until a 'gluten window' (see glossary) forms.

Grab another bowl about the same size, and spray it with canola oil. Transfer the dough to the bowl, cover with a tea towel and allow to rest and rise (prove) for a minimum of 2 hours or ideally overnight.

Divide the dough into 6 equal portions and shape into balls. Rub the softened butter in your hands and coat each dough ball, then cover and allow to rest for 2–3 hours.

Add 1 teaspoon of peanut oil to a clean, flat surface, then use your hands to press and push out each ball of dough until it's a very thin sheet, forming a rectangle.

Heat a wok over high heat and add 3–5 centimetres of oil. Once the oil is hot, add one piece of the roti dough in a spinning motion to create a 'snail' effect and cook, constantly basting with the oil on both sides, for 30–60 seconds or until golden brown.

Remove from the heat and drain on paper towel, then crush the roti in your hands. Repeat with the remaining roti dough. Serve immediately with the curry.

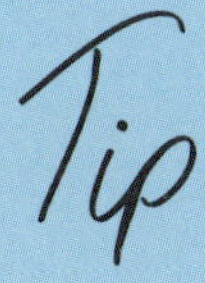

Making roti canai is a slow process because of the amount of gluten the dough needs to develop. Don't be tempted to cut the resting times, because you'll end up with dry and tough roti (bad) rather than flaky and golden roti (good).

Sweet Treats

A lot of the recipes I share in this chapter are those I created in my home kitchen when I was a kid, and sold to cafes around Melbourne as I was building up my business. Over the years, I have refined these sweet goodies into what they are today. You can find many of them at my Bistro Morgan Bakehouse, or you can make them at home!

Homemade Tim Tams

Total prep time	Total cook time	Makes	Difficulty
45 minutes, plus chilling time	15 minutes	12	☆☆★

Whose favourite biscuit isn't a Tim Tam? Here is my take on this classic.

For the biscuits

- 230 grams unsalted butter, room temperature
- ¾ cup (150g) brown sugar
- ½ cup (110g) caster sugar
- 2 free-range eggs, room temperature
- 3¼ cups (485g) plain flour
- 2 tablespoons cornflour
- 2 teaspoons bi-carb soda
- ¼ cup (25g) cocoa powder

For the chocolate buttercream

- 90 grams unsalted butter, room temperature
- 2 cups (250g) icing sugar, sifted
- ⅓ cup (30g) cocoa powder, sifted
- 1 tablespoon malted milk powder
- ⅓ cup (80ml) full-cream milk

For the chocolate topping

- 200 grams chocolate (50–60% cocoa solids)
- 1 tablespoon coconut oil

To make the biscuits

In a bowl of a stand mixer fitted with a paddle attachment, mix the butter, brown sugar and caster sugar for 3 minutes, then add the eggs and mix for a further 5 minutes until the mixture looks smooth, pale and fluffy. Add the plain flour, cornflour, bi-carb soda and cocoa powder, and mix until just combined.

Press the dough out into a disc (this will make it easier to roll out later), wrap in a tea towel and refrigerate for at least 1 hour or ideally overnight.

Preheat the oven to 180°C. Line a baking tray with baking paper.

Roll out the dough between 2 sheets of baking paper into a 5-millimetre-thick sheet. Remove the sheets, and cut the dough into 4 x 8-centimetre rectangles, and place on your baking tray. Bake for 10–12 minutes, then transfer to a wire rack and allow the biscuits to cool completely.

To make the chocolate buttercream

In the bowl of a stand mixer fitted with a paddle attachment, mix the butter for 2 minutes or until smooth. Add the icing sugar, cocoa powder and malted milk powder, and mix on medium speed for 3 minutes or until smooth and fluffy. With the mixer running on low speed, slowly pour in the milk and continue mixing for 2 minutes or until the mixture is well combined, scraping down the sides as needed. Transfer the mixture to a piping bag fitted with a 1-centimetre nozzle.

To make the chocolate topping

In a bowl over a double boiler, combine the chocolate and coconut oil and stir continuously until you have a smooth mixture. (Alternatively, you can melt the mixture in the microwave, stirring in 30-second intervals, until it is smooth.)

To assemble

Pipe the buttercream filling onto a biscuit and place another biscuit on top to create a 'sandwich'. Over a wire rack, spoon over the chocolate topping over the top and sides and allow to set.

Lemon Delicious Pudding

Total prep time	Total cook time	Serves	Difficulty
20 minutes	1 hour	4	☆☆★

This is my dad's all-time favourite dessert; every year he asks me to make it for his birthday. When I was younger I always refused because it's a really straightforward dish, but it has since become one of my favourite comfort desserts too. So, Dad, this one's for you.

80 grams unsalted butter, softened

4 free-range eggs, separated, room temperature

2 cups (440g) caster sugar

2 cups (500ml) full-cream milk

zest of 1 lemon

juice of 4–5 lemons (about 200ml)

½ cup (75g) self-raising flour, sifted

icing sugar, to dust

good-quality vanilla ice cream, to serve

Preheat the oven to 160°C. Grease an 18-centimetre round baking dish.

In an electric mixer fitted with a paddle attachment, combine the butter, egg yolks and caster sugar, and beat until light and creamy. Add the milk, lemon juice and zest, and mix for a further 2 minutes on low speed. Remove from the mixer and fold in the flour using a wooden spoon or spatula. Transfer to another bowl and set aside.

Wash and dry the mixer bowl thoroughly. Use the electric mixer fitted with a whisk attachment to beat the egg whites until soft peaks form. Use a spoon to fold the egg whites into the lemon batter and mix gently to combine, taking care not to remove any excess air bubbles from the egg whites. Pour the batter into the prepared baking dish, stand the dish in a shallow pan of cold water and bake for 60–70 minutes or until golden brown on the top.

Dust with icing sugar and serve with vanilla ice cream.

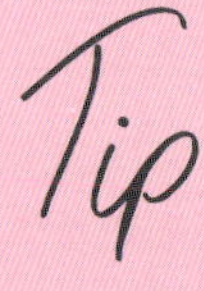

Ensure the bowl you whip the egg whites in is super clean – any fat or moisture will affect how much air can be added to the egg whites and ultimately the rise of the pudding.

Chocolate Soufflé

Total prep time	Total cook time	Makes	Difficulty
30 minutes	15 minutes	4	☆☆☆

This chocolate soufflé reminds me fondly of my time in Paris. The light, fluffy texture pairs brilliantly with the sweet vanilla sauce.

For the soufflés

¾ cup (180 ml) full-cream milk

2 free-range egg yolks

⅓ cup (75g) caster sugar

1 tablespoon plain flour

½ cup (50g) cocoa powder, sifted

240 grams good-quality dark chocolate, broken into bite-sized pieces

10 free-range egg whites, room temperature

pinch of cream of tartar

icing sugar, to dust

For the vanilla sauce

3 free-range egg yolks

1 tablespoon plain flour

¼ cup (55g) caster sugar

¾ cup (190ml) full-cream milk

½ cup (115ml) cream

1 teaspoon vanilla-bean paste

Preheat the oven to 200°C. Grease and sugar 4 x 250-millimetre soufflé ramekins or mini copper pots.

To make the soufflés

In a small saucepan over low heat, slowly bring the milk to a boil. In a bowl, whisk the egg yolks, half the caster sugar and the flour until light and fluffy. Slowly pour the hot milk over the egg yolks, and whisk until combined. Return the mixture to the saucepan and stir for 2 minutes or until the mixture coats the back of a spoon. Remove from the heat and whisk in the cocoa powder and chocolate. Set aside to cool while you prepare the egg whites.

In the bowl of an electric mixer fitted with a whisk attachment, add the egg whites and cream of tartar, and beat until stiff peaks form, then gradually add the remaining caster sugar and beat for 2 minutes until glossy.

Using a wooden spoon, carefully fold the whipped egg whites into the chocolate base. Divide evenly among the ramekins, and bake for 15 minutes or until the edges are set and the centre just wobbles when you give the pan a light tap.

To make the vanilla sauce

In a bowl, combine the egg yolks, flour and caster sugar, and whisk for 2–3 minutes or until pale and creamy. In a small saucepan, combine the milk, cream and vanilla, and bring the mixture to a boil over medium heat. Gradually add this to the egg-yolk mixture while stirring constantly for 1 minute, then return the combined mixture to the saucepan and stir over low heat until the mixture coats the back of a spoon. Transfer to a serving jug ready to serve.

My Perfect Pavlova

Total prep time	Total cook time	Serves	Difficulty
45 minutes	80 minutes, plus 4–5 hours' cooling time in oven	6–8	☆☆★

When I auditioned for *Junior MasterChef Australia* in 2010, I was a bundle of nerves. I had to take one signature dish I had made at home, and I chose my pavlova. I missed out on the TV show, but this recipe has always served me well, from winning baking contests at my primary-school fete to countless family desserts. It's a classic!

For the pavlova

4 free-range egg whites, room temperature

1 cup (220g) caster sugar

2 tablespoons cornflour

2 teaspoons white vinegar

For the topping

seeds of 1 vanilla bean

2⅓ cups (585ml) thickened cream

2 tablespoons icing sugar, sifted

your favourite fruits, to serve; mine are passionfruit, raspberries, blueberries, kiwi fruit and strawberries

small/micro mint leaves, to serve

To make the pavlova

Preheat the oven to 160°C.

Place the egg whites in the bowl of an electric mixer fitted with a whisk attachment, and beat for 2–3 minutes or until stiff peaks form. You should be able to hold the bowl upside down without the egg whites moving. This step is crucial for the formation of the pavlova's structure.

Slowly add the caster sugar, roughly ¼ cup at a time, while whisking on high speed for 3 minutes. Add the cornflour and vinegar, and whisk for a further minute on high speed. Your mixture should now look glossy, smooth and thick.

On a piece of baking paper, draw a 20-centimetre circle, then flip the paper over onto a baking tray so the circle is on the bottom side. Spoon the pavlova mixture into the centre of the circle, then use a smooth knife or a spatula to carefully push the mixture out to the edges. You can either go for a super-crisp sharp edge (great for a formal occasion such as Christmas lunch) or a more rustic approach (perfect for a Sunday barbie).

Place the pavlova mixture into the oven, reduce the temperature immediately to 140°C and bake for 80 minutes, ensuring you do not open the oven door during the cooking process. Keep the door closed while you allow the pavlova to cool completely in the oven (4–5 hours).

Carefully remove the pavlova from the oven and peel off the baking paper, then transfer the pavlova to a serving platter. Using your hands, crack the top meringue layer so it falls down into the middle – this will avoid having a hollow gap when you serve the pav. Set the pavlova aside while you prepare the topping.

To make the topping

In a bowl, combine the cream, vanilla seeds and icing sugar. Mix with an electric mixer fitted with a whisk attachment for 1–2 minutes or until soft peaks form. Spoon the cream onto the pav and spread evenly over the top, then decorate with your favourite fruit and top with mint leaves. Serve immediately.

Cinnamon Tea Cake

Total prep time	Total cook time	Serves	Difficulty
20 minutes	45 minutes	6–8	★☆☆

When I was a kid, my great-grandmother – Nana Leo – would serve a cinnamon tea cake whenever I visited. I can't tell you how much I loved that cake! It wasn't until years later that I discovered her secret: packet mix! Packet-mix cakes are a great way to build confidence in the kitchen. The satisfaction of such a quick process is really rewarding, especially for kids. At the same time, it's super important as you progress to move away from these mixes and develop your bake-from-scratch skills. That's certainly what I did.

170 grams unsalted butter

1 cup (220g) caster sugar

1 teaspoon vanilla extract

3 free-range eggs

2 cups (300g) cake flour

1 tablespoon baking powder

2 teaspoons ground cinnamon

1 cup (250ml) full-cream milk

2 tablespoons caster sugar, to serve

1 teaspoon ground cinnamon, to serve

30 grams unsalted butter, melted, to serve

Preheat the oven to 180°C. Grease and line an 18-centimetre springform cake tin with butter and baking paper.

In the bowl of an electric mixer fitted with a paddle attachment, mix the butter and caster sugar on medium speed for 3–4 minutes or until the mixture is pale and fluffy. Add the vanilla and eggs, and mix on medium speed for 2 minutes. Add the flour, baking powder and cinnamon, and mix on low speed until everything is just combined. Pour in the milk and use a wooden spoon to gently mix it through.

Pour the mixture into the prepared cake tin, then bake for 35–45 minutes or until the top is golden brown. To test the cake, carefully insert a skewer into the centre – if the skewer comes out clean, your cake is ready.

In a small bowl, combine the caster sugar and cinnamon. While your cake is still warm, use a pastry brush to brush the melted butter over the top of the cake, then sprinkle the cinnamon sugar over the top.

Hot Chocolate with Homemade Marshmallows

Total prep time	Total cook time	Makes	Difficulty
1 hour, plus setting time for the marshmallows	10 minutes	1 hot chocolate, 24 marshmallows (leftovers can be stored in an airtight container for up to 2 weeks)	★★☆

This recipe is absolutely as decadent as it sounds. Once you try real hot chocolate, you'll never go back to powdered!

For the homemade marshmallows (you can also use store bought)

9 gelatine leaves

3 free-range egg whites, room temperature

1½ cups (330g) caster sugar

3 teaspoons liquid glucose

¾ cup (180ml) water

seeds of 1 vanilla bean

1 cup (120g) icing sugar, sifted

½ cup (75g) cornflour

For the hot chocolate (per mug)

30 grams dark chocolate

20 grams white chocolate

1 cup (250ml) full-cream milk

½ teaspoon cinnamon sugar

Special equipment

Sugar thermometer

To make the marshmallows

Line a baking tray (approximately 20 x 30 centimetres and 2 centimetres deep) with baking paper.

Soak the gelatine leaves in a bowl of cold water for 5–10 minutes or until soft.

Place the egg whites in the clean bowl of an electric mixer fitted with a whisk attachment, and beat them until soft peaks form.

Combine the caster sugar, liquid glucose and water in a saucepan. Cook over medium–high heat for 3–5 minutes or until the mixture reaches 118°C on a sugar thermometer. Once this syrup reaches 127°C, remove the gelatine leaves from the bowl and squeeze out any excess water, then quickly stir the leaves into the syrup, along with the vanilla seeds.

With the mixer running, add the syrup to the egg whites, and mix for 10 minutes or until the mixture is cool and thick. Transfer the mixture to your baking tray, then use a spatula or the back of a spoon to smooth over the top. Refrigerate for 2–3 hours until set.

In a bowl, combine the icing sugar and cornflour, and stir with a spoon to create the dusting sugar mix. Cut the set marshmallows into squares and dust with the dusting sugar.

To make the hot chocolate

In a saucepan over low heat, combine the chocolate, milk and cinnamon sugar. Vigorously stir the mixture for 4–5 minutes or until the milk just comes to a simmer (don't let it boil!). Pour the hot chocolate into a mug and serve with a marshmallow (or two). Toast the marshmallows over a flame first for an extra-sweet treat.

Fairy-Bread Lamingtons

Total prep time	Total cook time	Makes	Difficulty
45 minutes	30 minutes	8	☆☆★

I have combined two Aussie classics: fairy bread and lamingtons. The result is a beautifully fluffy fairy-bread cake dipped in the classic chocolate icing and coconut. On the outside it looks like a regular lamington, but one bite and it says otherwise.

For the cake

110 grams unsalted butter

1 cup (220g) caster sugar

¼ cup (50g) brown sugar

3 free-range eggs

⅓ cup (90ml) buttermilk

¼ cup (65ml) vegetable oil

1⅔ cups (250g) cake flour

1 teaspoon baking powder

¼ cup (50g) 100s & 1000s

For the cream-cheese frosting

40 grams unsalted butter, softened

¾ cups (90g) cream cheese, room temperature

1 cup (125g) icing sugar, sifted

For the chocolate icing

3¾ cups (470g) icing sugar, sifted

¼ cup (20g) cocoa powder

15 grams unsalted butter, melted

½ cup (125ml) boiling water

To assemble

½ cup (100g) 100s & 1000s

1 cup (80g) desiccated coconut

To make the cake

Preheat the oven to 160°C. Grease and line a 18 x 26-centimetre cake tin.

In the bowl of an electric mixer fitted with a paddle attachment, combine the butter, caster sugar and brown sugar, and mix for 2–3 minutes or until the mixture is pale and fluffy. Add the eggs, and mix for 2 minutes on medium speed. Reduce the mixer to low speed, then pour in the buttermilk and oil, and mix until it is smooth and fluffy. Add the flour, baking powder and 100s & 1000s, and mix on low speed until just combined.

Pour into the prepared cake tin and bake for 25–35 minutes or until the cake springs back when you gently touch it. Allow the cake to cool completely while you move on to the next steps.

To make the cream-cheese frosting

In a bowl, combine the butter and cream cheese, and mix with an electric mixer fitted with a paddle attachment until the mixture is smooth and fluffy. Add the icing sugar on low speed just to combine, then mix on high speed for 2 minutes.

To make the chocolate icing

In a bowl, combine the icing sugar, cocoa powder, butter and boiling water, and mix with an electric mixer fitted with a paddle attachment until smooth.

To assemble

Cut the cake into squares and then in half to separate the top and the bottom. Put the 100s and 1000s in a bowl, and the coconut in another. Spread a layer of cream-cheese frosting on half the cake squares, then top with the remaining squares to make lamingtons. Dip each lamington into the 100s & 1000s, and finally coconut, coating all sides as you go.

Coconut Ice Cream

Total prep time	Total cook time	Serves	Difficulty
30 minutes, plus churning/freezing time	15 minutes	4	☆☆★

Koh Samui has one of the most beautiful beaches I have ever seen – and the food on this island is just as good. There's a fishing village, Bophut, where hundreds of market stalls line the streets serving almost anything you can think of. Our go-to dessert when we visited was freshly made coconut ice cream served in a coconut shell and topped with peanuts. Here is my version.

- 1 cup (250ml) full-fat coconut milk
- 2 cups (500ml) full-fat coconut cream
- 4 free-range egg yolks
- ¾ cup (165g) caster sugar
- 4 coconut husks, to serve (optional)
- 2 tablespoons crushed peanuts, to serve

In a saucepan over low heat, combine the coconut milk and coconut cream, and stir the mixture as it comes to a boil.

In a medium bowl, combine the egg yolks and caster sugar, and use a whisk or an electric mixer to beat until pale and fluffy. Slowly pour the coconut mixture into the egg mixture while whisking continuously, then return the combined mixture back to the pot and stir over a low heat for 5 minutes.

Remove from the heat and refrigerate until very cold. Churn the cold custard in an ice-cream machine (time according to your machine; mine takes 20 minutes). If you don't have an ice-cream machine, pour your mixture into a container and leave it in the freezer for at least 6 hours, until the ice cream hardens, checking and stirring it with a spatula every 2 hours.

Once your ice cream is frozen, scoop into the coconut husks and top with crushed peanuts.

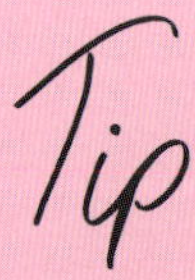

Coconut husks are available at most supermarkets, but you will need to remove the outer shell using a meat cleaver or a really heavy knife. This is an adults-only job!

Portuguese Custard Tarts

Total prep time	Total cook time	Makes	Difficulty
30 minutes	10 minutes	12	★★★

These tarts were one of my most popular creations when I first started to sell my baked goods to cafes in Melbourne as a kid.

½ cup (110g) caster sugar

⅓ cup (85ml) water

¼ cup (35g) plain flour

⅔ cup (170ml) full-cream milk

⅔ cup (170ml) cream

1 vanilla bean, split lengthways and seeds scraped

3 free-range egg yolks

1 sheet frozen puff pastry, just thawed

1 tablespoon cinnamon sugar

Preheat the oven to 220°C and grease a muffin tin with canola spray or butter.

In a saucepan over medium heat, combine the caster sugar and water, and bring it to a boil. Cook for 6 minutes, stirring occasionally to stop the mixture catching on the bottom.

While the sugar syrup is cooking, combine the flour and half the milk in a small bowl, and whisk until completely smooth.

Place the remaining milk along with the cream and vanilla bean and seeds in a saucepan over low heat and bring just to a boil – take care not to over-boil this mixture, because it will give the milk a burnt flavour. Remove the pan from the heat and slowly strain the mixture over the flour mixture in the bowl. Stir to combine, then add the egg yolks and mix again to combine. Finally, slowly pour in the sugar syrup to finish your custard. Set the mixture aside.

Dust a clean, dry surface with flour, then lay out the pastry sheet. Sprinkle the cinnamon sugar over the top, then carefully roll the pastry into a log. Cut into 12 even pieces, then use a rolling pin to roll out into rounds with an 8-centimetre diameter.

Press the pastry rounds into the muffin tin and three-quarters fill each one with custard. Bake for 10–12 minutes or until the custard just starts to blister. These are best enjoyed warm from the oven.

Chocolate Hazelnut Friands

Total prep time	Total cook time	Makes	Difficulty
20 minutes	15 minutes, plus cooling time	12	★★☆

These friands used to be one of my staples for supplying Melbourne cafes in the early days of Bistro Morgan. They're super moist and fluffy, and with the classic combo of hazelnut and chocolate I can almost guarantee you'll fall in love with them.

For the friands

6 free-range egg whites, at room temperature

1 cup (150g) plain flour

⅓ cup (35g) cocoa powder

1½ cups (240g) icing sugar

1 cup (100g) ground hazelnuts

200 grams unsalted butter, melted and cooled

extra icing sugar, to dust

extra cocoa powder, to dust

For the chocolate sauce, to serve (optional)

150 grams dark chocolate

½ cup (125ml) thickened cream

Preheat the oven to 200°C and grease 12 friand tins.

Place the egg whites in the bowl of an electric mixer fitted with a whisk attachment, and mix on high speed until really loose peaks form.

In another bowl, sift in the flour, cocoa powder and icing sugar, and use a spoon to mix in the ground hazelnuts. Using the spoon, make a well in the centre, then add the egg whites and melted butter into the well, and mix gently to combine. Spoon the mixture evenly into the greased tins, and bake for 20–25 minutes. To test the friands, carefully insert a skewer into the centre – if the skewer comes out clean, the friands are ready.

If you are making the sauce, while the friands are cooking, melt the chocolate and cream together in a saucepan over low heat, stirring until smooth, then transfer to a bowl and serve with the friands.

Allow the friands to cool in the tin for 10 minutes before you transfer them to a wire rack. Once cooled, dust them with icing sugar and cocoa powder, and serve either as they are or with the chocolate sauce.

My Perfect Salted Caramel Shake

Total prep time 10 minutes, plus 1 hour cooling time for the caramel | Total cook time 10 minutes | Makes 1 shake; leftover caramel can be stored sealed in the fridge for up to a month | Difficulty ☆☆★

Nothing annoys me more than a warm, fluffy shake – follow my recipe for the perfect shake every time! These are a winner on their own or with pretty much any of the sweet snacks in this book.

For the salted caramel

1 cup (220g) caster sugar

¼ cup (65ml) water

55 grams unsalted butter, room temperature, cut into cubes

⅓ cup (85ml) thickened cream

1 teaspoon sea salt flakes (the smoked variety is best)

For the milkshake (per shake)

1 cup (250ml) full-cream milk, cold

4 large scoops (250g) good-quality vanilla-bean ice cream

2 tablespoons salted caramel

To make the salted caramel

In a saucepan over medium heat, add the caster sugar and then the water. Bring to a simmer (just below a boil), stirring every so often for 5 minutes or until the sugar has dissolved. Stop stirring and cook for a further 4–5 minutes or until it forms a smooth brown caramel. Take care not to burn the caramel – its colour should be amber rather than dark brown. (Be careful – this mixture will be super hot!)

Remove the pan from the heat and stir in the butter and cream, then whisk vigorously (but carefully; you are adding a cold liquid to an extremely hot mixture, and it might splatter) until completely combined. Allow the mixture to cool down slightly, then sprinkle in the salt. Set aside until it cools completely before using in the milkshake, or cover tightly and refrigerate.

To make the milkshake

In a blender, combine the milk, ice cream and your homemade salted caramel sauce, and blend until smooth (don't over-blend it, because this will make the milkshake warm and fluffy). Pour into a serving glass and enjoy immediately.

Homemade Doughnuts

Total prep time	Total cook time	Makes	Difficulty
30 minutes, plus proving and resting time	10 minutes	18	☆☆☆

My signature doughnut recipe takes up to three days to make; it's a slow process that has been developed over many years and is constantly evolving to ensure it's always the best it can be. So, I've created this simplified version here so you can create delicious doughnuts at home.

3 cups (480g) bread flour

¾ cup (165ml) buttermilk

1 teaspoon fine sea salt

7 grams dried yeast (15g fresh yeast)

2 free-range eggs

1 cup (275g) caster sugar

80 grams unsalted butter, softened

1 cup (220g) caster sugar, to dust

vegetable oil

In the bowl of an electric mixer fitted with a dough hook, combine the bread flour, buttermilk, salt, yeast, eggs and ¼ cup of the caster sugar, and mix for 10–15 minutes or until a 'gluten window' (see glossary) forms. Add the butter, and mix for 2–3 minutes or until combined.

Grab another bowl about the same size, and spray it with canola oil. Transfer the dough to the bowl, cover with a tea towel and allow to rest and rise (prove) for 1 hour or until it has doubled in size.

Line a baking tray with baking paper.

Turn the dough onto a lightly floured surface and divide into 18 equal portions. Using a circular motion with the palm of your hand, gently roll the dough into balls. Transfer the balls of dough to your baking tray, cover and allow to prove in a warm environment for 1–2 hours or until doubled in size.

While the doughnuts are proving, heat a deep fryer to 160°C (if you don't have a deep fryer, you can use a large pot half filled with vegetable oil; you will need a thermometer to ensure the oil stays at the correct temperature).

Once the doughnuts have doubled in size, use lightly floured hands to pick up each doughnut and very carefully add it to the oil (don't drop it in!), rounded-side down. Cook on both sides for 2 minutes or until golden brown. Carefully remove from the oil with a slotted spoon and allow to cool on a wire rack. Cook 1–2 doughnuts at a time. Once cool, dust with the remaining caster sugar and fill with your favourite fillings.

Gaytime Cake

Total prep time	Total cook time	Serves	Difficulty
2 hours, plus cooling time	45 minutes	6–8	☆☆☆

Golden Gaytime ice creams are iconically Australian, so whenever I bring this cake to a party it goes down a treat. This bad boy consists of a super-moist and fluffy caramel cake layered with a chocolate, caramel and vanilla frosting and topped with homemade honeycomb and a malted chocolate crumb. This recipe was originally inspired by Milk Bar Store's famous Birthday Cake.

Note on caramel:

1 quantity of my salted caramel (page 98) will be enough to cover all elements in this recipe.

For the salted caramel cake

115g unsalted butter, softened

1 cup (220g) caster sugar

¼ cup (55g) brown sugar

3 free-range eggs

½ cup (125ml) buttermilk

¼ cup (60ml) grapeseed oil

150 grams salted caramel (page 98)

1⅔ cups (250g) cake flour

½ teaspoon fine sea salt

1 teaspoon baking powder

For the honeycomb (you can also use store-bought Violet Crumble chocolate bars if preferred)

¼ cup (90g) honey

¼ cup (60ml) liquid glucose

1 cup (220g) caster sugar

¼ cup (60ml) water

1 tablespoon bi-carb soda, sifted

For the malted chocolate crumb

½ cup (110g) caster sugar

2 tablespoons brown sugar

⅔ cup (100g) cake flour

½ teaspoon baking powder

⅓ cup (35g) cocoa powder

1 tablespoon malted milk powder

¼ cup (60ml) grapeseed oil

For the frosting

400 grams unsalted butter, softened

1 cup (120g) cream cheese, room temperature

4 cups (500g) icing sugar

2 tablespoons liquid glucose (if you don't have glucose on hand you can omit it; the glucose just helps to achieve a nice shiny finish to the icing)

2 tablespoons cocoa powder

2 tablespoons salted caramel (page 98)

1 teaspoon imitation vanilla essence

For the caramel soak

¼ cup (60ml) full-cream milk

1 tablespoon salted caramel (page 98)

Special equipment to assemble the cake

15-centimetre springform cake tin

20-centimetre strip of acetate approximately 15 centimetres high

Pastry brush

PTO for the cooking steps

To make the salted caramel cake

Preheat the oven to 180°C. Grease and line a 30 x 20-centimetre baking tin with butter and baking paper.

In the bowl of an electric mixer fitted with a paddle attachment, mix the butter, caster sugar and brown sugar for 2–3 minutes or until the mixture is pale and fluffy. Add the eggs and mix for a further 3 minutes or until smooth. Carefully pour in the buttermilk, grapeseed oil and salted caramel, then mix on medium speed for a further 3 minutes or until smooth. Add the flour, salt and baking powder, and mix until just combined.

Pour the cake batter into the tin and bake for 30–35 minutes or until the cake is spongy and bounces back when you press it lightly. Set aside to cool completely.

To make the honeycomb

Line a baking tray with baking paper.

In a small saucepan, combine the honey, liquid glucose, caster sugar and water. Stir with a wooden spoon over a low heat until it comes to a boil, then continue to cook, stirring, for 1–2 minutes or until it reaches a caramel colour. Working quickly, remove the saucepan from the heat and stir in the bi-carb soda, being careful because the mixture will foam up. Transfer the mixture to the baking tray, and set it aside to cool for at least 1 hour. Once cooled, break the honeycomb into small pieces.

To make the malted chocolate crumb

Preheat the oven to 180°C. Line a baking tray with baking paper.

In the bowl of an electric mixer fitted with a paddle attachment, combine the caster sugar, brown sugar, flour, baking powder, cocoa powder and malted milk powder, and mix on low speed for 1 minute or until the ingredients are combined. Add the grapeseed oil, and mix on low speed until combined; the mixture should now be very dry and crumbly. Transfer the mixture to the baking tray and bake for 15 minutes. Remove from the oven, and allow the crumbs to cool completely.

To make the frosting

In the bowl of an electric mixer fitted with a paddle attachment, combine the butter and cream cheese, and mix on medium speed for 1–2 minutes or until the mixture is smooth. Mix in the icing sugar and liquid glucose (if using) on low speed just to combine, then mix on high speed for 4–5 minutes or until you have a stark-white, fluffy frosting. Divide the mixture evenly between three bowls. In the first bowl, use an electric mixer or a wooden spoon to mix in the cocoa powder to create a chocolate frosting. In the second bowl, mix in the salted caramel to create a caramel frosting. And in the third bowl, mix in the vanilla essence to create a vanilla frosting.

To make the caramel soak

In a bowl, whisk together the milk and salted caramel until combined.

To assemble

Carefully flip the cake out of the tin onto a clean chopping board, and peel off the baking paper. Using a 15-centimetre springform cake tin to guide you (the ring, not the base), use a sharp knife to cut out two rounds – these are the top two layers of your cake. The remaining cake will form the bottom layer.

Clean the cake tin ring and place it in the centre of your serving platter (trust me, you won't want to move this cake once it's assembled), and use the strip of acetate to line the inside of the tin.

Using the back of a spoon, push the cake scraps inside the ring to create the bottom layer. Then, use a pastry brush to coat the cake with the caramel soak. Top with the chocolate frosting, using a spatula to spread it evenly and right to the edge of the tin, then add a generous sprinkling of the malted chocolate crumbs and honeycomb. Top with the middle layer of cake, then repeat the process with the soak, the caramel frosting and the crumbs. Finally, add the top layer of cake, brush on the soak again and spread on the vanilla frosting, ensuring this layer is perfectly smooth because it will be the main layer on show, then top with another generous sprinkling of crumb and honeycomb pieces. Carefully transfer the cake to the fridge and chill for at least 2 hours or up until overnight. Remove from the fridge, and remove the tin and the acetate 1 hour prior to serving.

Chocolate Chip Cookies

Total prep time 20 minutes | Total cook time 15 minutes | Makes 10 | Difficulty ☆☆★

My signature choc-chip cookies can become your signature too!

230 grams unsalted butter, softened, cut into cubes

¾ cup (165g) firmly packed brown sugar

½ cup (110g) caster sugar

2 free-range eggs

2½ cups (375g) plain flour

1 tablespoon cornflour

1 teaspoon bi-carb soda

½ teaspoon fine sea salt

350 grams good-quality dark chocolate chips (50–60% cocoa solids)

1 tablespoon sea salt flakes, to top the cookies (optional)

Preheat the oven to 200°C. Line a baking tray with baking paper.

In the bowl of a stand mixer fitted with a paddle attachment, combine the butter, brown sugar and caster sugar, and mix for 2 minutes or until the mixture is light and fluffy.

Use a silicone spatula to scrape down the sides and bottom of the bowl. Add the eggs, and mix on high speed until the mixture is light and fluffy (and no longer looks separated). Add the plain flour, cornflour and bi-carb soda, and mix on the lowest speed until all the flour is just incorporated. Add the chocolate chips, and mix on the lowest speed until the chocolate chips are evenly incorporated into the dough.

Use your hands to mix the dough – it should now be quite sticky – to make sure the chocolate chips are evenly distributed. Divide the dough evenly into 10 balls. Make sure to keep it loose, because the cookies should be light and airy. Place the cookies on the lined baking tray (don't press them down), leaving at least 5 centimetres between each cookie for them to spread. Top each cookie with a sprinkle of sea salt (optional) and bake for 15–18 minutes or until golden brown.

Remove from the oven, allow to cool on the tray for 10 minutes and then transfer to a wire rack to finish cooling. These cookies are best enjoyed the day you bake them, but you can keep any leftovers in an airtight container for up to 2 days.

Cinnamon Scrolls

Total prep time 1 hour, plus resting and proving time | Total cook time 20 minutes | Makes 12 | Difficulty ☆☆★

These cinnamon scrolls officially came into my life when we rebranded the store as Bistro Morgan Bakehouse. They're super fluffy with a lovely cinnamon filling and a vanilla glaze – I mean, what's not to love here!

For the dough

3¼ cups (520g) bread flour

1 cup (250ml) full-cream milk

7 grams dried yeast (15g fresh yeast)

¼ cup (55g) caster sugar

1 teaspoon fine sea salt

75 grams unsalted butter, softened

For the cinnamon buttercream filling

200 grams unsalted butter, softened

¼ cup (50g) brown sugar

1 tablespoon ground cinnamon

For the glaze

2 cups (250g) icing sugar, sifted

2 teaspoons liquid glucose (or golden syrup)

2 tablespoons full-cream milk

1 tablespoon water

1 tablespoon cream

seeds of 1 vanilla bean

To make the dough

In the bowl of an electric mixer fitted with a dough hook, combine the flour, milk, yeast, caster sugar and salt, and mix on low speed for 3 minutes. Use a silicone spatula to scrape down the sides of the bowl to make sure all the flour has been incorporated, then mix for a further 10–15 minutes or until a 'gluten window' (see glossary) forms. Add the butter, and mix for 2 minutes or until there are no chunks of butter left.

Grab another bowl about the same size, and spray it with canola oil. Transfer the dough to the bowl, cover with a tea towel and allow to rest and rise (prove) for 1 hour or until it has doubled in size.

To make the cinnamon buttercream filling

Line a baking tray with baking paper.

Combine the butter, brown sugar and cinnamon in the bowl of an electric mixer fitted with a paddle attachment, and mix on medium speed for 4–5 minutes or until light and fluffy. Transfer the dough to a floured work surface and roll out the dough to a 35 x 25-centimetre rectangle. Spread a thin layer of cinnamon buttercream over the dough, then roll the dough to create a large 'log'. Using a sharp knife, cut in 3–4-centimetre pieces.

PTO for more cooking steps

Place the cinnamon scrolls on the baking tray, cut-side up, leaving a 3-centimetre gap (this will ensure they bake into each other and get that nice, soft edge). Cover with a clean tea towel and allow to prove for 1 hour or until doubled in size and the scrolls are touching each other.

Preheat the oven to 180°C while the scrolls finish proving.

Bake the scrolls for 15–20 minutes, checking frequently to ensure the scrolls don't burn. We want them to be a nice light-golden brown.

To make the glaze

In a bowl of an electric mixer fitted with a paddle attachment, combine the glaze ingredients and mix on high speed for 3 minutes.

To glaze the scrolls

To ensure the scrolls stay nice and fluffy right up until you serve them, it's best to not separate them until you're ready to eat. I've found it's best to flip them onto a wire rack to glaze and serve.

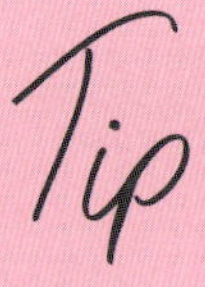

Most scroll recipes just sprinkle cinnamon sugar in the middle, but by filling these with cinnamon buttercream we get a sweeter and moister filling. So, that means even more deliciousness!

Homemade Churros

Total prep time	Total cook time	Makes	Difficulty
30 minutes	5 minutes	15–20	☆☆☆

When I walked across the US border to visit Mexico for the day and discovered a whole street lined with traditional churros carts, I grabbed a bag – they were so good I can't even put it into words. I've had a crack at re-creating this amazing memory.

For the churros

½ cup (110g) caster sugar

1 tablespoon ground cinnamon

½ teaspoon ground nutmeg

1 cup (250ml) water

120 grams unsalted butter

¼ cup (55g) caster sugar, extra

¾ cup (115g) plain flour

1 teaspoon salt

2 free-range eggs

1 cup vegetable oil

For the Nutella chocolate sauce

½ cup (145g) Nutella

¼ cup (60ml) full-cream milk

To make the churros

In a shallow, wide bowl, combine ½ cup (110g) caster sugar with the cinnamon and nutmeg to create the cinnamon sugar coating, and set aside.

In a saucepan over medium–low heat, combine the water, butter, remaining caster sugar, flour and salt, and cook, stirring with a wooden spoon, until a thick paste forms, then continue to mix for 2–3 minutes or until the mixture completely comes away from the side of the saucepan.

Transfer the mixture to the bowl of an electric mixer fitted with a whisk attachment, and mix on medium speed for 1 minute to slightly cool the mixture. With the mixer running, add the eggs and mix on medium speed for 2–3 minutes or until the mixture is smooth and shiny. This is choux pastry. Transfer the mixture to a piping bag fitted with a 0.5–1-centimetre star tip.

Add the vegetable oil to a deep fry pan over medium heat and heat to 180°C. Pipe 8–10-centimetre lengths of batter into the oil using a pair of scissors to snip the end off each churro. Fry, turning, for 4–5 minutes or until golden brown. Remove the churros from the oil and toss them in the cinnamon and nutmeg coating. Serve immediately with the hot Nutella sauce.

To make the Nutella chocolate sauce

In a small saucepan over medium heat, combine the Nutella and milk, and stir until hot and smooth.

Strawberry Shortcake Panna Cotta

Total prep time	Total cook time	Serves	Difficulty
45 minutes	6 hours' setting time	6	☆☆★

Panna cotta has such a stigma – but it's not nearly as challenging to make as you might think. I promise, if you take your time, you'll be able to nail this dish first time round.

For the panna cotta

5 gelatine leaves

2 punnets (500g) strawberries, tops removed

½ cup (125ml) full-cream milk

⅓ cup (75g) caster sugar

1 teaspoon vanilla extract

1½ cups (375ml) thickened cream

For the walnut shortbread crumb

125g unsalted butter, softened

¼ cup (55g) caster sugar

1 cup (150g) plain flour, sifted

¼ cup (50g) rice flour, sifted

½ cup (50g) walnuts

For the strawberry coulis

2 punnets (500g) strawberries, tops removed

½ cup (60g) icing sugar

½ teaspoon lemon juice

To serve

small/micro mint leaves

To make the panna cotta

Grease 6 dariole moulds or ramekins with butter or oil spray.

Soak the gelatine leaves in a bowl of cold water for 5–10 minutes or until soft.

While the gelatine leaves are soaking, place the strawberries in the bowl of a food processor, and blitz until the mixture is very smooth. Then, carefully pour it into a fine sieve and push the puree through, to capture any final seeds or lumps. Discard the seeds and lumps, but transfer the strawberry puree to a saucepan. Add the milk and caster sugar, and cook over medium–low heat for 2 minutes or until the mixture reaches 60°C.

Remove the gelatine leaves from the bowl and squeeze out any excess water. Put ice cubes into a large bowl next to the stove and sit a medium bowl over the ice.

Remove the pan of strawberry mixture from the heat and quickly stir in the drained gelatine leaves. While stirring constantly, add the vanilla and cream, then transfer the mixture to the bowl set over ice. Stir frequently for 10 minutes or until the mixture cools to 15–20°C (if you don't have a thermometer, just cool it to room temperature).

Divide the mixture evenly among the 6 greased ramekins, and refrigerate for at least 6 hours or ideally overnight.

PTO for more cooking steps

To make the walnut shortbread crumb

Preheat the oven to 160°C. Line a 20–30-centimetre baking tray with baking paper.

Lightly flour a clean, dry surface, then transfer your dough, and knead gently until smooth.

Sprinkle plain flour on a clean, dry surface, then transfer your dough, and knead gently until smooth.

Push the dough onto your baking tray, using a spoon to spread it evenly, and press down into the corners to ensure the whole tray is covered, then bake for 40 minutes or until lightly golden.

Remove the shortbread crumb from the oven and allow it to cool completely.

When it is cool, add the shortbread in batches to the bowl of a food processor and pulse until a coarse crumb forms. Set aside while you make the strawberry coulis.

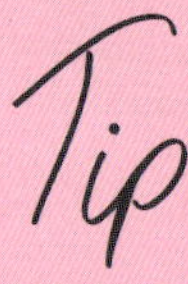

Panna cotta is notorious for not setting, so take your time and don't rush the setting process. One of the best things about panna cotta is that it can be made two days ahead of time, so try to plan ahead if you can, because this will ensure the panna cotta sets properly.

And . . . the walnut shortbread crumb might look dry when you make it, but this is how it should look! It's dryness is what makes it able to turn into the beautiful crumb we see on the final dish.

To make the strawberry coulis

Wash the strawberries and cut them into quarters. Place them in a saucepan with the icing sugar and lemon juice over a medium heat, and cook for 5–10 minutes or until the strawberries have completely collapsed. Transfer the strawberries to the bowl of a food processor, and blitz until you have a smooth sauce. Carefully pour the sauce through a fine sieve and push the liquid through; this captures any final seeds or lumps. Discard the seeds and lumps, and set the strawberry coulis aside to cool.

To serve

Remove the panna cotta from the fridge. Carefully tip out a panna cotta onto the centre of each serving plate, then drizzle the strawberry coulis around it and spoon on the shortbread crumb. Garnish with mint leaves.

Go-To Brownies

Total prep time	Total cook time	Makes	Difficulty
15 minutes	30 minutes	12 pieces	★☆☆

When I first started to bake sweet treats, these brownies were requested everywhere I went. They're perfect to make if you are running short on time, because they're so simple – just throw everything in a bowl and mix, and 30 minutes later you've got the best gooey, chocolatey brownies ever.

4 free-range eggs, room temperature

240 grams unsalted butter, melted

¾ cup (75g) cocoa powder, sifted

2 cups (440g) caster sugar

1 cup (150g) plain flour, sifted

½ cup (85g) dark choc chips (50–60% cocoa solids)

icing sugar, to serve (optional)

Preheat the oven to 180°C and line a baking tray with baking paper.

In a large mixing bowl, crack the eggs and whisk until they are pale and fluffy. Add the remaining brownie ingredients except for the icing sugar, and mix with a wooden spoon until everything is just combined. Make sure you don't over-mix the batter, because this will cause tough, dry brownies – and we want the opposite!

Pour the brownie mixture into your baking tray, using your spoon to spread it evenly and press down into the corners to ensure the whole tray is covered, then bake for 30–35 minutes or until the middle is just wobbly. (You can check by pressing a fork – or your finger – against it.)

Remove from the oven and allow to cool completely, then dust with icing sugar to serve if you like a little extra sweetness.

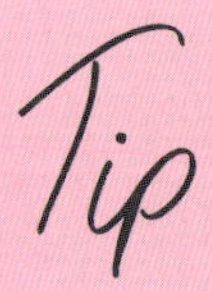

Use a baking tray around 18 x 25 centimetres.

Anytime

These recipes are some of my absolute favourites. They are delicious treats that can be enjoyed across the day, for a meal or even a late-night snack.

Chicken Satay

Total prep time	Total cook time	Serves	Difficulty
1 hour, plus marinating time	15 minutes	6	★★★

A visit to Kuala Lumpur, Malaysia, is never complete without a trip to Petaling Street, a bustling market strip that comes alive at night. My favourite dish will always be chicken satay cooked on an open grill until the marinated chicken caramelises and is then lathered in a sweet and salty peanut satay sauce – it doesn't get much better than this.

For the satay

4 cloves garlic

1 large knob ginger, peeled and thinly sliced

1 knob fresh turmeric (or 1 tablespoon ground turmeric)

6 shallots

3 teaspoons coriander seeds

2 teaspoons ground cumin

1 teaspoon black pepper

1 teaspoon fine sea salt

1 kilogram chicken thighs, cut into bite-sized pieces

For the satay sauce

4 dried red chillies

1 tablespoon coriander seeds

roots from 1 bunch coriander

1 tablespoon ground cumin

½ stalk lemongrass, white part only, finely chopped

1-centimetre piece galangal

2 kaffir lime leaves

1 shallot, finely chopped

2 cloves garlic, peeled and crushed

1 tablespoon water

1¼ cups (310ml) coconut cream

2 tablespoons palm sugar

½ cup (125ml) chicken stock

½ cup (60g) finely ground peanuts

1 teaspoon fish sauce

sea salt and freshly ground black pepper, to taste

To serve

coriander leaves

peanuts, roasted

chilli flakes

bird's-eye chilli, thinly sliced

To make the satay

In the bowl of a food processor, combine all the satay ingredients except for the chicken, and blitz on high speed until a paste forms. Rub the mixture onto the chicken, then let the chicken rest in the fridge for a minimum of 2 hours or ideally overnight.

To make the satay sauce

In the bowl of a food processor, combine the chillies, coriander seeds, coriander roots, cumin, lemongrass, galangal, lime leaves, shallot and garlic, and blitz until a thick paste forms, then add the water and blitz to combine.

Heat the coconut cream in a saucepan over medium heat for 1 minute, then add the paste and fry over low heat for 4–5 minutes until it smells amazing. Add the palm sugar, stock, ground peanuts and fish sauce, and cook for a further 5 minutes. Taste the sauce, and add salt and pepper if you think it needs more seasoning, then cook on low heat for 10 minutes. Remove from the heat and allow it to sit for 1 hour, then serve at room temperature with the chicken. (Any remaining satay sauce can be stored in an airtight jar in the fridge for up to a month.)

To serve

Thread the chicken onto skewers and chargrill over medium–high heat for 2 minutes on both sides or until cooked through. Garnish with coriander leaves, peanuts and chilli, and serve immediately with a side of satay sauce.

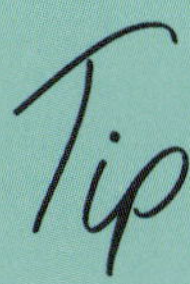

If you're running short on time, you can always use store-bought satay sauce, but my homemade version is so much tastier!

Jalapeño Croquettes

Total prep time	Total cook time	Serves	Difficulty
30 minutes, plus chilling time	10 minutes	4 as a starter	☆☆☆

The food culture in Spain is, simply, next level. Influences from Portugal and France, as well as Mexico, combine to create an amazing cuisine that packs a tasty punch. I especially love San Sebastian, an area famous for its pintxo, small tapas-style dishes usually served on skewers. Here is one of my favourites.

70 grams unsalted butter, chopped into cubes

⅔ cup (100g) plain flour

2 teaspoons cornflour

2 cups (500ml) full-cream milk

80 grams pickled jalapeños, roughly chopped

1 cup (100g) grated mozzarella or Monterey Jack

sea salt and freshly ground black pepper, to season

2 free-range eggs

¼ cup (60ml) full-cream milk

¼ cup (35g) plain flour, extra

2 cups (200g) panko breadcrumbs

vegetable oil

sea salt, to season

baby pickles, to serve

In a saucepan over medium–low heat, combine the butter, plain flour and cornflour. Stir with a wooden spoon for 2 minutes to create a roux, then add the 2 cups (500ml) milk and whisk until smooth. Continue to cook, stirring, for 10 minutes or until the sauce is very thick. Remove from the heat, and stir in the jalapeños and cheese, and season with salt and pepper. Transfer to a container with a lid, and refrigerate for at least 5 hours or ideally overnight.

In a small bowl, add the eggs and the ¼ cup (60ml) milk and whisk until combined. In another small bowl, add the flour. In another bowl, add the breadcrumbs.

Roll the cooled croquette mixture into 12 even sausage-shaped pieces. Dip each croquette in the flour, then in the egg wash and then in the breadcrumbs. To double-crumb the croquettes, dip them back into the egg wash, then back into the breadcrumbs. Return them to the fridge for 1 hour.

Heat a deep-fryer or around 5 centimetres of vegetable oil in a deep-fry pan to 160°C. Deep-fry the croquettes for 3–4 minutes or until dark-golden brown, then remove them from the oil with a slotted spoon, drain on paper towel and season with sea salt. Top with a baby pickle and insert a skewer (toothpick) to serve. Serve hot.

Chicken Tacos

Total prep time	Total cook time	Makes	Difficulty
30 minutes, plus marinating time	15 minutes	6	★★☆

There's something so satisfying about sitting down to some really good tacos. I love plating all the individual elements up in share bowls in the centre of the table and allowing my guests to build their own tacos.

For the marinade

½ cup (65g) chopped coriander leaves

⅓ cup (80ml) extra-virgin olive oil

¼ cup (60ml) soy sauce

juice of 1 lime

4 cloves garlic, peeled and crushed

1 jalapeño, seeded and finely chopped

1 teaspoon ground cumin

sea salt and freshly ground black pepper, to taste

300 grams chicken tenderloins

For the pickled cabbage

1½ cups (500g) sliced red cabbage

2 tablespoons (35g) caster sugar

1 teaspoon salt

½ cup (125ml) rice-wine vinegar (or apple-cider vinegar)

For the tacos

1 tablespoon olive oil

6 small flour tortillas, toasted

1 corn on the cob following my Chilli and Lime Charred Corn recipe (page 144), kernels sliced off

1 avocado, seeded and thinly sliced

2 tablespoons sriracha Kewpie mayonnaise (you can find this in most supermarkets)

lime wedges, to serve

coriander leaves, to serve

To make the marinade

In a large bowl, combine the coriander leaves, extra-virgin olive oil, soy sauce, lime juice, garlic, jalapeño, cumin, salt and pepper. Add the chicken, and mix to coat in the marinade. Set aside to marinate for a minimum of 3 hours or ideally overnight.

To make the pickled cabbage

In a small saucepan, combine the cabbage, caster sugar, salt and rice-wine vinegar. Place the saucepan over low heat and stir until it comes to a boil. Remove from the heat and allow it to cool completely.

To make the tacos

Place a pan over medium–high heat and add the olive oil. Add the marinated chicken, and cook for 2–3 minutes, then turn and cook for a further 2–3 minutes or until golden brown. Remove the chicken from the pan and cut into cubes. Assemble the tacos with the chicken, pickled cabbage, corn kernels, avocado, a drizzle of mayo, a squeeze of lime and top with coriander.

Chicken Schnitzel Sandwich

Total prep time	Total cook time	Serves	Difficulty
15 minutes	15 minutes	4	★★★

Chicken schnitzel is one of my favourite foods – it's so simple but just so more-ish. Here, I've taken the classic chicken schnitzel and made it into an epic sandwich using my potato buns.

1 cup (340g) sliced red cabbage

1 tablespoon caster sugar

½ teaspoon salt

¾ cup (180ml) rice-wine vinegar (or apple-cider vinegar)

2 tablespoons plain flour

1 free-range egg

1 tablespoon full-cream milk

1 cup (100g) panko breadcrumbs

vegetable oil

1 chicken breast, beaten with a meat mallet until 2-centimetres thick, cut into 10-centimetre 'patties'

1 quantity of my potato buns (page 140), or store-bought soft milk buns

Kewpie mayonnaise (you can find this in most supermarkets)

1 cup shredded iceberg lettuce

4 slices Monterey Jack cheese

pickles

In a small saucepan, combine the cabbage, caster sugar, salt and rice-wine vinegar. Place the saucepan over low heat and stir until it comes to a boil. Remove from the heat and allow it to cool completely.

Set up three bowls. In the first bowl, put the flour. In the second bowl, whisk the egg with the milk. In the third bowl, put the breadcrumbs.

Pour 1 centimetre of vegetable oil into a fry pan over medium–low heat. While the oil is heating, dip the chicken 'patties' one by one into the flour, then into the egg until well coated, and finally into the breadcrumbs. Add the crumbed schnitzels to the pan and cook for 2–3 minutes, then turn them over and cook for another 2–3 minutes – essentially you want them all to be golden brown and crispy all over.

While the schnitzels are frying, split and toast the buns.

To assemble the sandwiches, layer the bottom half of each bun with the mayo, lettuce, chicken, cheese, pickled cabbage and pickles and finally add the top bun.

Ultimate Beef Pie

Total prep time	Total cook time	Makes	Difficulty
1 hour, plus resting time	3½ hours	8	★★★

This is your classic pie, loaded with real, slow-cooked beef and homemade shortcrust pastry. Top it with tomato sauce for the perfect combo.

For the filling

750 grams chuck steak, beef cheeks or gravy beef

½ cup (60g) cornflour

salt, to season

1 tablespoon olive oil

2 carrots, peeled and grated

2 sticks celery, grated

2 shallots, finely chopped

2 cloves garlic, peeled and crushed

1 tablespoon balsamic vinegar

1 tablespoon tomato paste

2 cups (500ml) beef stock

½ cup (125ml) good-quality red wine

1 dried bay leaf

2 sprigs thyme, leaves picked

For the shortcrust pastry

1⅔ cups (250 grams) plain flour

200 grams unsalted butter, cold, cut into cubes

½ cup (125ml) sour cream

For the pies

3 frozen puff-pastry sheets, just thawed

3 free-range eggs, lightly beaten

sesame seeds (optional)

tomato sauce, to serve

Tip

Be super careful not to overwork your shortcrust pastry. Allow it to rest as soon as it comes together. It will become tough if overworked, and we want the opposite! And, don't make the pie crust too thin, otherwise it will break when you pick up the pie.

To make the filling

Preheat the oven to 140°C.

In a bowl, dust the beef with cornflour and season with salt. Add the olive oil to an ovenproof casserole dish, then transfer the beef to the dish and place over high heat. Fry the beef in batches for 2–3 minutes or until crispy and brown, then remove the beef from the dish and set aside.

Add the carrot, celery, shallot, garlic and balsamic vinegar to the casserole dish. Place over low heat, and cook, stirring with a wooden spoon, for 5 minutes. Add the tomato paste and cook for 1 minute. Return the beef and its juices to the casserole dish, along with the stock, wine, bay leaf and thyme. Place a lid on the casserole dish and cook in the oven for 3 hours.

To make the shortcrust pastry

In the bowl of a food processor, combine the flour and butter. Pulse for 30–60 seconds or until the mixture resembles breadcrumbs. With the food processor running slowly, pour in the sour cream, and blitz until it just forms together into a ball of dough.

Press the dough out into a disc (this will make it easier to roll out later), wrap in a tea towel and refrigerate for at least 1–2 hours prior to using.

Preheat the oven to 180°C. Grease 8 pie tins.

On a clean, dry surface, use a rolling pin to roll out the dough to 3–5 millimetres thick. Then cut the dough into 15-centimetre rounds and press into the greased pie tins.

Line with baking paper and add baking weights or rice. Bake for 20 minutes. Remove the weights or rice and bake for a further 5 minutes or until the base is dry and lightly golden. Remove from the oven and allow to cool.

To make the pies

Preheat the oven to 200°C.

Fill the cooled base with the meat mixture. Cut 8-centimetre rounds (or the diameter of your pie tin) from the puff pastry and place over the mixture to make a lid, pressing the edges together to seal. Cut a tiny cross in the top of each pie with a small, sharp knife and brush with the beaten eggs, then scatter with sesame seeds, if using. Bake for 25–30 minutes or until golden brown and flaky. Serve hot with tomato sauce.

Cheesy Herb-Stuffed Pretzels

Total prep time 30 minutes, plus resting and proving time | Total cook time 20 minutes | Makes 10 | Difficulty ★★★

I made these pretzels one afternoon when experimenting in the kitchen trying to come up with some ideas for my next cooking video. I threw a couple of ingredients together and the next thing I knew, my Cheesy Herb-Stuffed Pretzels were born.

For the pretzels

1½ cups (375ml) warm water

7 grams dried yeast (15g fresh yeast)

2 tablespoons caster sugar

1 teaspoon fine sea salt

1 tablespoon finely chopped rosemary

1 tablespoon finely chopped thyme

3½ cups (560g) bread flour

90 grams unsalted butter, softened

2 cups (240g) freshly grated mozzarella

4 cups (1L) water

¼ cup (60g) bi-carb soda

melted unsalted butter, to brush over

For the egg wash

1 free-range egg

2 tablespoons full-cream milk

For the topping

1 cup (80g) grated parmesan

½ teaspoon sea salt

½ teaspoon garlic powder

1 tablespoon finely chopped rosemary

1 tablespoon finely chopped thyme

To make the pretzels

In the bowl of an electric mixer fitted with a dough hook, combine the water, yeast, caster sugar, salt, rosemary, thyme and bread flour, and mix on low speed for 10 minutes or until a 'gluten window' (see glossary) forms. Add the butter and mix for 2 minutes.

Grab another bowl about the same size, and spray it with canola oil. Transfer the dough to the bowl, cover with a tea towel and allow to rest and rise (prove) for 1 hour or until it has doubled in size.

Preheat the oven to 200°C. Line a baking tray with baking paper.

Transfer the dough to a clean, dry surface. With your hands, divide the dough into 10 equal pieces. Roll each piece out into a 25–30-centimetre 'rope' and use a rolling pin to flatten it. Scatter 2 tablespoons of the mozzarella over each piece of dough, then roll to enclose the cheese. Roll the dough up to form a pretzel.

In a large saucepan over medium heat, add the water and bi-carb soda, and bring to a boil.

Dip each pretzel in the bi-carb soda 'bath' for 30 seconds, then drain and add to the baking tray.

In a bowl, combine the egg and milk. Brush the pretzels with the egg wash and bake for 15 minutes.

To make the topping

Combine all the topping ingredients in a bowl.

Transfer the pretzels to a wire rack. Use a pastry brush to brush the pretzels with the melted butter, then sprinkle the topping over the hot pretzels.

Chicken Nuggets

Total prep time	Total cook time	Serves	Difficulty
30 minutes, plus marinating time	15 minutes	4	★★★

Chicken nuggets were one of the few things I would eat when I was a kid, so it would be a sin to not include my take on this timeless classic. So often nugget recipes include minced chicken, but I preferred to use real chicken breast.

For the nuggets

½ cup (125ml) buttermilk

¼ cup (60ml) pickle juice

pinch of sea salt

3 chicken breasts or thighs, cut into nuggets

1 cup (150g) cornflour

1 tablespoon paprika

1 tablespoon garlic powder

1 tablespoon onion powder

1 teaspoon pepper

1 teaspoon dried oregano

1 teaspoon dried basil

1 teaspoon mustard powder

1 cup (250ml) vegetable oil

chicken salt, to season

For the sweet-and-sour sauce

½ cup (160g) apricot jam

2 tablespoons liquid glucose

2 tablespoons water

1 tablespoon white-wine vinegar

1 teaspoon chicken stock powder

½ teaspoon soy sauce

½ teaspoon yellow American mustard

½ teaspoon garlic powder

In a bowl, combine the buttermilk, pickle juice and salt, then add the chicken, and mix to coat the chicken. Allow the chicken to sit in the marinade at room temperature for at least 30 minutes or ideally overnight.

While the chicken is marinating, make the sauce. In the bowl of a food processer, combine all the sauce ingredients and blitz until smooth. Transfer to a saucepan over medium heat and stir for 2–3 minutes or until the mixture comes to a boil and becomes clear. Pour through a sieve into a bowl and set aside to cool.

In another bowl, combine the cornflour, paprika, garlic and onion powders, pepper, dried oregano, dried basil and the mustard powder.

Heat a deep fry pan over medium heat and add the vegetable oil. Drain the chicken from the buttermilk and dust generously with the dry seasoning mix, then place carefully in the hot oil. Fry for 2–3 minutes or until golden and crispy. Drain on paper towel and toss with chicken salt, then serve with the cooled sweet-and-sour sauce.

My Perfect Burger

Total prep time	Total cook time	Makes	Difficulty
1 hour, plus resting and proving time	30 minutes	1 burger (and 12 buns)	★★★

This is a go-to dish for hanging with my mates. They would probably buy milk or brioche buns, which is totally fine, but I like to make mine from scratch. I love to serve this with a side of The Best Chips Ever (page 162).

For the tangzhong paste

¼ cup (35g) bread flour

¼ cup (60ml) water

⅓ cup (85ml) full-cream milk

For the potato buns

¾ cup (180ml) full-cream milk

14 grams dried yeast (28g fresh yeast)

3 cups (480g) bread flour

2 teaspoons fine sea salt

¼ cup (55g) caster sugar

2 free-range eggs

1 free-range egg yolk

150 grams mashed potato (you can use instant potato-mash powder: mix together ½ cup boiling water and ⅓ cup potato-mash powder in a bowl and set aside for 10 minutes before using)

60 grams unsalted butter, softened

For the egg wash

1 free-range egg

1 tablespoon full-cream milk

For the special sauce

½ cup (150g) mayonnaise

1 tablespoon tomato sauce

1 tablespoon American mustard

¼ onion, peeled and finely chopped

2 pickles, finely chopped

¼ teaspoon garlic powder

¼ teaspoon paprika

For the burger

1 tablespoon vegetable oil

240 grams beef mince, refrigerated

pinch of sea salt and freshly ground black pepper

2 slices Monterey Jack cheese

2 rashers streaky bacon

green oak lettuce

4 pickles, sliced

1 tomato, sliced

PTO for the cooking steps

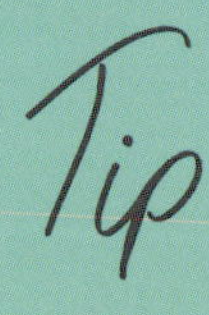

Tangzhong is a Japanese method used to increase the moisture content in a dough by gelatinising the flour so the dough is still workable. I've borrowed this technique to make these potato buns extra light and fluffy.

To make the tangzhong paste

In a small saucepan over low heat, combine all the tangzhong ingredients and stir vigorously for 4–5 minutes or until a thick paste forms. Remove from the heat.

To make the potato buns

In the bowl of an electric mixer fitted with a dough hook, combine all the potato bun ingredients except the butter and add the tangzhong paste, then mix on low speed for 10 minutes or until a 'gluten window' (see glossary) forms. Add the butter, and mix for 2 minutes.

Grab another bowl about the same size, and spray it with canola oil. Transfer the dough to the bowl, cover with a tea towel and allow to rest and rise (prove) for 1 hour or until it has doubled in size.

Line a baking tray with baking paper.

Lightly flour a clean, dry surface. Divide the dough into 12 equal portions. Using a circular motion with the palm of your hand, gently roll each piece of dough to create a ball. Place the balls on a lined baking tray with at least 5–6 centimetres between each ball. Cover with a clean tea towel, and allow to prove in a warm area for 1–1½ hours or until doubled in size.

Preheat the oven to 180°C.

To make the egg wash

In a bowl, combine the egg and milk, and mix with a spoon until combined.

Once the buns have proved, use a pastry brush to brush them generously with the egg wash, then bake for 15–20 minutes or until the buns are dark-golden brown. Allow to cool completely.

To make the special sauce

In a bowl, combine all the sauce ingredients and mix with a spoon until combined.

To make the burger

Heat a large fry pan over high heat until super hot, then add the vegetable oil. Remove your beef from the fridge and divide it into 2 equal balls. Sprinkle with salt and pepper, then place the balls in the fry pan, leaving room for them to be squished down. Cook them for 30 seconds and then use a heavy pan or dish to squish them all the way down until they can't be squished anymore. Cook for a further 3–4 minutes or until the edges start to turn brown. Flip them over and immediately place a slice of cheese on top of each patty. Cook for 1–2 minutes or until the cheese melts.

While the burgers are cooking, place a seperate pan over medium heat and cook the bacon for 2 minutes or until crispy.

To assemble the burger

Cut the bun in half. In the same pan you used to fry the patties, add the halved bun cut-side down and toast on high heat for 1 minute or until crispy. Remove from the heat, then add a lettuce leaf, a spoonful of sauce, a patty, a rasher of bacon, the second patty, the pickles, some tomato slices, more sauce and then, finally, the top of the bun.

Chilli and Lime Charred Corn

Total prep time	Total cook time	Serves	Difficulty
20 minutes	10 minutes	4	☆☆★

Walking the streets and beaches of Bali wasn't complete without a piping hot cob of corn in your hand. Here is my take on this classic street-food treat to re-create at home.

For the chilli butter

250 grams unsalted butter, room temperature

2 cloves garlic, peeled and crushed

zest of 1 lime

1 bird's-eye chilli, finely chopped

1 bunch coriander, finely chopped

1 teaspoon ground cumin seeds

sea salt and freshly ground black pepper

For the corn

4 corn cobs (ideally still in the husk to maximise freshness)

Kewpie mayonnaise, to serve (you can find this in most supermarkets)

finely chopped coriander, to serve

finely sliced chilli, to serve

grated parmesan, to serve

lime wedges, to serve

To make the chilli butter

Combine all the chilli butter ingredients in a bowl, and mix to combine. Set aside.

To make the corn

Preheat a grill to high and allow it to heat for at least 10 minutes. Remove the husks from the corn and then add the cobs to the grill. Use a pastry brush to coat each piece with the chilli butter generously. Cook for 10 minutes or until the corn is charred all over, continuing to brush generously with the butter and turning often.

Top the charred corn with a drizzle of mayo, and scatter on the coriander, chilli and cheese. Serve immediately with the lime wedges.

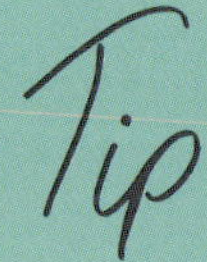

A barbecue grill works best for this recipe, but you can also use a heavy-based, cast-iron chargrill pan.

Semi-Sourdough Loaf

Total prep time	Total cook time	Makes	Difficulty
2 hours, plus resting and proving time (the starter is made the day prior)	30 minutes	2	★★★

I've been baking sourdough since I was nine years old. It's a labour of love, to say the least: maintaining a starter means feeding it every day and looking after it – it's almost like having a pet. In my 'cheat's' semi-sourdough we get over this by making a starter the day prior and giving it a hand with some yeast. Enjoy!

For the starter

¾ cup (120g) bread flour

3 grams dried yeast (or 6g fresh yeast)

⅔ cup (165ml) warm water (room temperature)

For the dough

3 cups (480g) bread flour

5 grams dried yeast (or 10g fresh yeast)

1 cup (250ml) warm water (room temperature)

3 teaspoons fine sea salt

Special equipment

Dutch oven

To make the starter (1 day prior)

In a large jar with a lid, mix together the flour, yeast and water until they are thoroughly combined – the mixture should have the consistency of pancake batter. Put the lid on the jar, and allow the starter to rest at room temperature for 12–15 hours.

To make the dough

In the bowl of an electric mixer fitted with a dough hook, mix the flour, yeast, water and all of the starter. Mix on low speed for 3 minutes, then use a silicone spatula to scrape down the bowl to make sure all the flour has been incorporated. Knead for a further 10–15 minutes or until a 'gluten window' (see glossary) forms.

Grab another bowl about the same size, and spray it with canola oil. Transfer the dough to the bowl, cover with a tea towel and allow to rest and rise (prove) for 2 hours or until it has doubled in size.

Transfer the dough to a clean, dry surface. Sprinkle the salt over the dough, then knead by hand for around 3 minutes to incorporate the salt into the dough. Return the dough to the bowl and allow to prove for a further hour.

Divide the dough into 2 equal portions (they should be around 500 grams each). Gently fold the edges of each piece of dough into the centre to form a ball and turn them seam-side down on the bench. Allow to rest for 15 minutes.

To shape the dough, working with one piece at a time, turn the dough seam-side up and pat to remove any air bubbles. Position your hands with your fingertips touching at the bottom of the dough. Using the sides of your hands, lift up the bottom of the dough and fold it so it covers two-thirds of the dough, then fold the top over and bring it down so it covers the folded dough. Repeat with the other dough portion. Transfer each portion to a sheet of baking paper.

Allow the dough to rest and rise (prove) for 1 hour. To test if it is ready, gently press the dough with your finger – if the impression remains, your dough is ready.

While the dough is proving, preheat the oven to 200°C. Place a Dutch oven and its lid in the oven to heat up.

Using a sharp knife, score the loaf by carefully making a single cut down the centre. Transfer the loaf to your Dutch oven, using the baking paper, then spray with water and cover with the lid. Bake for 20 minutes.

Using oven mitts, remove the loaf from the Dutch oven and transfer to a baking tray. Place it in the oven and bake for a further 15 minutes or until the bread sounds hollow when tapped. Remove the loaf from the oven and let it cool completely on a cooling rack before you slice it.

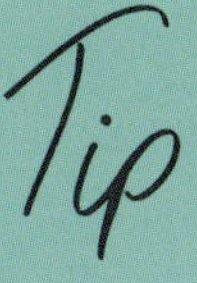

Sourdough is a truly amazing thing. It's yeast in natural form – live bacteria that are different in every environment, which is why every sourdough loaf is different.

Hanoi-Style Spring Rolls

Total prep time	Total cook time	Makes	Difficulty
45 minutes	5 minutes	10	★★★

Vietnam one of my favourite places in the world. Vietnamese food is fresh and balanced; it's all about the yin and yang. Ingredients such as lemongrass, chilli and coriander are so versatile yet so distinct in their flavour that it is truly a craft to be able to use these in the precise amounts seen in Vietnamese cuisine.

For the spring rolls

350 grams pork shoulder, minced (your butcher can do this for you, or you can use regular store-bought pork mince)

1 small jicama (turnip), peeled and grated

2 free-range eggs

4 dried mushrooms (preferably wood-ear), soaked in warm water for 20 minutes then thinly sliced

100 grams vermicelli noodles, soaked in boiling water for 10 minutes

1 cup (180g) bean sprouts

1 shallot, finely sliced

1 clove garlic, peeled and crushed

1 tablespoon fish sauce

10 large round rice-paper sheets

1 free-range egg, lightly beaten, extra

peanut oil (or vegetable oil)

Vietnamese mint and iceberg lettuce, to serve

For the nuoc mam dipping sauce

⅔ cup (150g) caster sugar

1 cup (250ml) hot water

2 red chillies, finely chopped

5 cloves garlic, peeled and finely chopped

¼ cup (60ml) rice-wine vinegar

¼ cup (60ml) fish sauce

PTO for the cooking steps

Tip

Using rice paper instead of spring-roll pastry results in a more traditional, Hanoi-style spring roll. They are simply a crunchier and tastier option. Also, ensure you take your time when rolling the spring rolls, and don't go crazy with the filling – if you put in too much and don't seal them properly, they will burst in the fryer.

To make the spring rolls

In a bowl, combine the minced pork, jicama, eggs, mushroom, vermicelli noodles, bean sprouts, shallot, garlic and fish sauce. Mix the ingredients until they are well combined.

Pour some warm water into a wide bowl. Dip a rice-paper roll wrapper in the water for a second (don't soak it, because it will become waterlogged and impossible to roll), then remove it and place half of another sheet on top. This is to create an extra layer to strengthen the roll.

Place 2 tablespoons of the filling on the bottom third of the wrapper. Lightly squeeze the mixture to remove any air bubbles and form the mixture into a log. Brush the wrapper with egg, fold the sides in and roll into a spring-roll shape. Repeat with the remaining rolls.

To make the nuoc mam dipping sauce

Dissolve the caster sugar in the hot water, then add the remaining sauce ingredients and mix well.

To serve

Heat the oil in a deep fryer or around 5 centimetres in a deep-fry pan to 180°C. Add the spring rolls and fry for 3–4 minutes, rolling them in the oil, or until golden brown. Remove with a slotted spoon and drain on paper towel. Serve hot with nuoc mam dipping sauce, Vietnamese mint and iceberg lettuce.

Cheesy Garlic Pull-Apart

Total prep time	Total cook time	Makes	Difficulty
10 minutes	20 minutes	1	★★★

Sometimes the best kind of recipes are fun, quick and easy, and that's certainly the case with my Cheesy Garlic Pull-Apart.

125 grams unsalted butter

2 cloves garlic, peeled and crushed

2 tablespoons finely chopped parsley

pinch of sea salt

1 semi-sourdough loaf (ideally my version, page 146)

4 slices Monterey Jack cheese

Preheat the oven to 180°C.

In a bowl, combine the butter, garlic, parsley and salt, and stir well to form garlic butter.

With a bread knife, cut the sourdough loaf into cubes but don't cut all the way through to the base. Open up the cracks and carefully stuff each crack with cheese. Spread the garlic butter over the top of the loaf. Wrap the loaf in foil, and bake for 20 minutes.

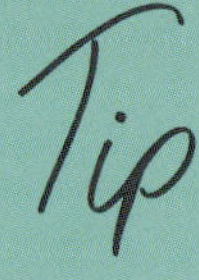

Ensure you generously 'stuff' the cuts in the loaf with the cheese so you end up with a super-gooey cheesy pull-apart.

Korean Fried Chicken

Total prep time	Total cook time	Serves	Difficulty
30 minutes, plus brine time	15 minutes	4	★★★

Korean fried chicken is my ultimate comfort food. This dish combines the classic crispy fried chicken we all know and love with an unbelievably flavoursome sauce. It doesn't get much better than this!

For the chicken brine

⅓ cup (80ml) rice-wine vinegar

2 cloves garlic, peeled and grated

30 grams ginger, peeled and grated

pinch of sea salt flakes and freshly ground black pepper

800 grams chicken – your preferred cut: wings, thighs or drumsticks

For the sauce

⅓ cup (80ml) gochujang (you can find it at most supermarkets)

2 tablespoons tomato sauce

2 tablespoons dark soy sauce

4 cloves garlic, peeled and grated

30 grams ginger, peeled and grated

2 tablespoons mirin

¼ cup (90g) honey

1 tablespoon oyster sauce

1 tablespoon rice-wine vinegar

For the fried chicken

vegetable oil

potato flour

sesame seeds, chilli flakes, sliced fresh chilli and coriander leaves, to garnish

To brine the chicken

In a large bowl, combine the rice-wine vinegar, garlic, ginger, salt and pepper, and mix until combined. Carefully place the chicken in the brine, turning to coat it, then refrigerate for a minimum of 2 hours or ideally overnight. Remove the chicken from the fridge an hour prior to cooking.

To make the sauce

Combine all the sauce ingredients in a saucepan over medium--low heat. Bring the mixture to a boil, then remove it from the heat and set aside until needed.

To make the fried chicken

Heat a deep-fryer or half fill a heavy, deep saucepan with vegetable oil to 160°C (you will need a thermometer to ensure the oil stays at the correct temperature). Place a wire rack over a tray lined with paper towel to drain the chicken.

Working in batches, coat the marinated chicken in the potato flour and then carefully place it in the deep-fryer or saucepan and cook for 5 minutes. Remove with a slotted spoon and drain on your wire rack, letting the oil drip through to the tray. Increase the oil temperature to 190°C and cook the chicken a second time in batches for a further 4 minutes or until golden and crispy, then drain on the rack and place in a bowl. Pour over the sauce and toss to combine, then garnish with the sesame seeds, chilli and coriander. Serve immediately.

Empanadas

Total prep time	Total cook time	Makes	Difficulty
1 hour, plus resting time	15 minutes	12	★★☆

Walking through the streets of Spain is never complete without a piping hot empanada. Enjoy these ones at home.

For the dough

3 cups (450g) plain flour

1 teaspoon fine sea salt

1 teaspoon baking powder

110 grams unsalted butter, cold, cut into cubes

¾ cup (190ml) ice-cold water

1 free-range egg, lightly beaten

For the filling

1 tablespoon extra-virgin olive oil

1 brown onion, peeled and finely chopped

2 cloves garlic, peeled and crushed

500 grams beef mince

1 tablespoon tomato paste

1 teaspoon dried oregano

1 teaspoon ground cumin

½ teaspoon smoked paprika

½ can (200g) diced tomatoes

¼ cup (25g) pickled jalapeños, finely chopped

sea salt and freshly ground black pepper, to season

For the empanadas

1½ cups (150g) grated cheddar

1 cup (100g) grated mozzarella

1 free-range egg

1 tablespoon full-cream milk

sour cream, to serve

sweet chilli sauce, to serve

finely chopped coriander, to garnish

To make the dough

In a large bowl, combine the flour, salt and baking powder. Add the butter, and rub the mixture with your fingertips until it resembles breadcrumbs. Add the water and egg, and use a wooden spoon to mix until a dough forms.

Lightly flour a clean, dry surface, then transfer your dough and knead for 3–4 minutes. Wrap in a tea towel and refrigerate for at least 1 hour or ideally overnight.

To make the filling

Add the extra-virgin olive oil, onion and garlic to a large fry pan over medium heat, and cook for 3–4 minutes or until it is soft and smells amazing. Add the beef and cook, using a wooden spoon to break up the mince, for 2–3 minutes or until brown, then drain any excess fat. Add the tomato paste, oregano, cumin and paprika, and stir to combine. Add the tomato and jalapeños, and cook until the mixture just comes to a boil. Taste for seasoning, and add salt and pepper if it needs it. Remove from the heat and allow to cool slightly.

To make the empanadas

Preheat the oven to 180°C and line a baking tray with baking paper.

Combine the cheeses in a bowl and set aside.

Remove the dough from the fridge and roll out half to 5–6 millimetres thick. Using an 8-centimetre round cookie cutter, cut out rounds. Repeat with the remaining dough.

Use a pastry brush to brush the outer edge of the dough with water, then place 2 tablespoons of the filling in the centre and top with a generous handful of the cheeses. Fold the dough in half over the filling and use a fork to seal the edges.

In a bowl, whisk the egg and milk until combined.

Add the sealed empanadas to the lined tray and brush with the egg wash. Bake for 20–25 minutes or until golden brown. Serve immediately with the sour cream and sweet chilli sauce and garnish with the coriander.

Garlic Bread Grilled Cheese

Total prep time	Total cook time	Makes	Difficulty
10 minutes	5 minutes	1	★★★

Two of my favourite comfort foods combined into one dish, need I say more? I love this creation for many reasons, but mainly because it's so simple, so easy and can be enjoyed at any time.

20 grams unsalted butter, room temperature

1 clove garlic, peeled and crushed

pinch of sea salt

1 teaspoon finely chopped parsley

2 thick slices sourdough bread (ideally my version, page 146)

3 slices cheese (Monterey Jack is my favourite, but you can also use a mix of mozzarella and cheddar)

1 tablespoon vegetable oil

sea salt flakes, to serve (optional)

In a bowl, combine the butter, garlic, salt and parsley, and stir well to form garlic butter. Generously butter one side of each slice of bread; these will be the outside of the sandwich. Then, place the cheese slices on the unbuttered side of one slice of bread, then add the other slice of bread to form a sandwich, with the butter on the outside.

Heat a fry pan over medium–low heat. When the pan is warm, add the vegetable oil, and then place the sandwich butter-side down in the pan and cover with a lid (this will allow the cheese to melt nicely). Cook on each side for 2–3 minutes or until golden brown. Sprinkle sea salt flakes over the top to serve, if you like.

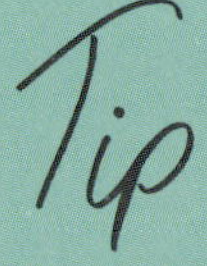

You can add meats such as ham or pastrami to this if you want to enhance the flavour even more.

The Best Chips Ever

Total prep time	Total cook time	Serves	Difficulty
45 minutes, plus 15 minutes' soaking time	20 minutes	4	☆☆☆

These chips are legit the best you will ever taste. They pair perfectly with Steak Frites (page 26), My Perfect Burger (page 140), Ultimate Beef Pie (page 132), Chicken Schnitzel Sandwich (page 130), Korean Fried Chicken (page 156) – or on their own they make the ideal afternoon or late-night snack.

1 kilogram King Edward potatoes

generous pinch of sea salt

1 litre sunflower oil

freshly ground black pepper

1 tablespoon finely chopped thyme leaves

1 tablespoon finely chopped rosemary leaves

smoked sea salt flakes, to season

Peel the potatoes and cut into your preferred chip size and shape, placing the chips into a large bowl of ice-cold water while you work. Soak the chips in the ice water for 15 minutes to remove excess starch (this helps create super-crispy chips), then rinse them again with fresh water. Place the chips in a large saucepan over medium–low heat, add enough water to cover the chips and the salt. Bring to a boil, then reduce to a simmer (just below a boil) and cook for 6–8 minutes or until you can just poke a fork through them (ensure you do not over-boil the potatoes at this stage, because it will make them almost impossible to fry without falling apart).

Remove the saucepan from the heat and drain the water. Transfer the chips to a baking tray lined with paper towel to absorb the excess water. This is crucial, because otherwise when you place the chips in the deep-fryer, the water left on the chips will boil in the hot oil.

Heat a deep-fryer or half fill a heavy, deep saucepan with vegetable oil to 150°C (you will need a thermometer to ensure the oil stays at the correct temperature). Add the chips in batches (take care not to overload the fryer) and fry for approximately 4 minutes or until they just form a coating.

Remove the chips from the oil with a slotted spoon and allow to drain completely on a wire rack. Then increase the fryer temperature to 180°C. Fry the chips for a second time, this time for 5–7 minutes or until golden brown and crunchy. Transfer the chips to a bowl lined with paper towel. Sprinkle with salt, pepper, thyme and rosemary leaves and toss to combine. Enjoy!

Chicken Apple Sandwiches

Total prep time	Total cook time	Makes	Difficulty
20 minutes	20 minutes, plus cooling time	4	★☆☆

My pet hate for school lunches was a dry sandwich. With my Chicken Apple Sandwiches you'll never have to worry about that. Oh, and I promise the apple does work in this!

- 2 chicken breast fillets
- 2 cups (500 millilitres) chicken stock
- 3 sprigs thyme, leaves picked
- 1 Granny Smith apple, peeled and grated
- 1 cup (300 grams) good-quality whole-egg mayonnaise
- sea salt and freshly ground black pepper, to taste
- 8 slices bread (ideally from my Semi-Sourdough Loaf, page 146)
- 30 grams unsalted butter, softened
- 1 cup shredded iceberg lettuce

Place the chicken, stock and thyme in a saucepan. Bring to a boil, then reduce heat and cook for 10 minutes. Keep the chicken in the stock to cool for 30 minutes, then remove the chicken and cut into small cubes. Add the chicken to a bowl along with the apple and mayo, stir to combine and season to taste with salt and pepper.

Heat a chargrill pan over high heat until hot. Lightly butter 8 bread slices. Place the bread buttered-side down and grill for 1 minute or until char marks appear on the bread. Remove from the heat and add the chicken mixture to 4 of the slices. Top with a handful of lettuce, sandwich together, cut in half and serve immediately.

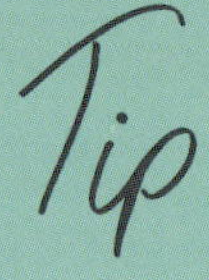

Squeeze some of the excess juice from the apple before adding to the filling mix so it doesn't make it too wet.

Hummus with Crispy Chorizo and Yoghurt Flatbread

Total prep time 45 minutes, plus resting and proving time | Total cook time 10 minutes | Serves 4 | Difficulty ★★☆

This is one of my favourite starters to any dinner. The flatbread is also awesome as a side dish to a main course.

For the yoghurt flatbread

¾ cup (210g) unsweetened Greek yoghurt

1½ cups (240g) bread flour

7 grams dried yeast (15g fresh yeast)

1 teaspoon salt

1 teaspoon caster sugar

1 tablespoon olive oil

2 tablespoons melted unsalted butter

For the hummus

1 x 420-gram can chickpeas, drained and rinsed

juice of 1 large lemon (approximately ¼ cup, 60ml)

¼ cup (60g) tahini

1 clove garlic

2 tablespoons extra-virgin olive oil

1 teaspoon ground cumin

40 grams ice

salt, to taste

paprika, to serve

For the crispy chorizo

2 dried chorizo sausages, cases removed and meat roughly chopped

1 tablespoon olive oil

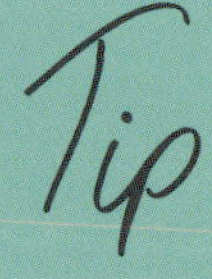

Adding ice cubes to the blender gives the hummus a freshly churned ice cream-like texture.

To make the yoghurt flatbread

In the bowl of an electric mixer fitted with a dough hook, combine the yoghurt, bread flour, yeast, salt and caster sugar, and mix for 10–15 minutes or until a 'gluten window' (see glossary) forms.

Grab another bowl about the same size, and spray it with canola oil. Transfer the dough to the bowl, cover with a tea towel and allow to rest and rise (prove) for 1 hour or until it has doubled in size.

To make the hummus

In a food processor, combine the chickpeas, lemon juice, tahini, garlic, extra-virgin olive oil, cumin, ice and salt, and blend for 1 minute or until smooth. Spoon into a bowl ready to serve.

To make the crispy chorizo

Place the chorizo in a food processor, and process for 1 minute or until a course crumb is formed. Heat a fry pan with the olive oil over medium heat, add the chorizo and cook, stirring, for 4–5 minutes or until the chorizo is crispy and crunchy. Remove the chorizo from the pan and drain on a plate lined with paper towel.

To make the flatbread

Lightly flour a clean, dry surface, then transfer your dough. Using your hands, push down the proved dough and divide into 4 equal pieces, then push them out into approximately 12-centimetre rounds.

Heat a large fry pan (a cast-iron skillet is ideal) over medium heat with the olive oil, then add the flatbread and cook for 3 minutes, then turn over and cook for a further 3 minutes or until golden brown. Remove from the heat to a plate and brush with the melted butter. Cover with a tea towel while you cook the remaining flatbreads.

To serve

Top the hummus with the crispy chorizo, and sprinkle over the paprika. Arrange the flatbread with the chorizo hummus on a serving platter, and enjoy.

If you are starting out on your cooking journey, good for you! Here are a few tips to help get you through the common processes that will help make everything smoother. And remember to have fun!

Baking/pastry weights

Baking weights are used to keep a pastry crust from bubbling and shrinking away from the edge of a tin when blind baking (this is the process of baking a pastry crust without the filling in it). If you don't own baking weights, you can use raw rice.

Bread flour

Bread flour is a variety of regular white flour that is higher in protein than regular all-purpose flour. This assists in the formation of gluten structure in any yeast-based doughs.

Butter – salted vs unsalted

All butter starts life as unsalted, then the salted variety has salt added to it to increase flavour and shelf life. I prefer the unsalted variety because it allows you to add salt based on your personal preference.

Cake flour

Cake flour has less protein than plain (all-purpose) flour, which results in a lighter and fluffier cake. You can find cake flour in most supermarkets, but if you can't, you can substitute 2 tablespoons in every cup of plain flour with 2 tablespoons cornflour, then sift this mixture twice.

Deep-frying

Deep-frying is the process of cooking food by submerging it in hot oil. The easiest way to do this is to use a store-bought deep-fryer; it automatically regulates the temperature throughout the cooking process. If you don't have a deep-fryer, you can use a heavy, deep saucepan and half fill it with oil. Heat the oil to the desired temperature and monitor it with a thermometer. Always deep-fry in small batches and lower the ingredients into the oil and remove carefully.

Double boiler

A double boiler involves sitting a heatproof bowl over a pot of simmering water ensuring the water doesn't touch the bottom of the bowl. It's ideal for things such as melting chocolate. This also refers to a purpose-made piece of kitchen equipment that consists of two saucepans designed to sit one on top of the other.

Egg whites, whisking eggs

Soft peaks barely hold their shape and flop over when the whisk is lifted. Firm peaks stand straight up when the whisk is lifted. It's important to use a clean, dry bowl when whisking egg whites because any residual fat can ruin the egg whites' ability to whisk up. Room-temperature eggs help achieve a better end result and allow the egg whites to trap more air when whipping.

Eggs, separating

Separating eggs is the process by which the egg yolk is removed from the egg white. Over a bowl, you need to gently crack the egg and then pour the yolk from one half of the shell to the other as the egg white drips into the bowl below and the yolk remains in the shell. (You will likely need to do this a few times to get all the white away from the yolk.) It can be a juggling act! It's super important not to get any egg yolk in egg whites that are going to be whisked (for a soufflé or pavlova, for example), because the fat in the yolks stops the whites from being able to trap the air and form the light and fluffy texture that is so important in the formation of these dishes.

Emulsify

To emulsify is to combine two ingredients that do not ordinarily mix easily. This is usually a fat (for example, olive oil or butter) and a water-based liquid such as vinegar. You will see an example of this in my béarnaise sauce from my Steak Frites recipe.

Frenched

This is a decorative way to present a piece of meat with a bone. The bone is stripped of all fat and sinew. Your butcher can do this for you.

Gelatine leaves

This is a setting agent that comes in both powder and leaf form. The leaves are the easiest way to use gelatine and are my preferred form, and you can find these in supermarkets. Ensure you soak them as instructed in my recipes prior to use.

'Gluten window'

This is when you can pull dough apart to make a transparent 'window' without the dough tearing at all – it means the dough has formed sufficient gluten structure. This is key in all yeast-based doughs. (See photo on page 175.)

Kewpie mayonnaise

Kewpie is mayonnaise of Japanese origin. It is smoother and creamier than regular store-bought mayo, and it has a distinct flavour that I love. It also comes in a Sriracha variety; I use both throughout my recipes. You can buy Kewpie mayo at most supermarkets, but if you're unable to source this, you can substitute it with regular mayonnaise.

Kipfler potatoes

One of my favourite variety of potato, kipflers are small to medium in size and are long, narrow, and have a finger-like shape. They are the ultimate roasting potato and are available from most fruit and vegetable stores.

Kneading

Kneading is the process of working dough to build gluten structures. It can be done by hand or in a stand mixer with a dough hook. To knead by hand, place the dough on a floured surface, then press and stretch it away from you with the heel of your hand, then fold it over and rotate 90 degrees – then repeat until a gluten window forms (see glossary entry and the photo opposite).

Liquid glucose

Liquid glucose is basically sugar in liquid form. I use it in my recipes to help achieve a nice shine to the finished product. You will find it in most supermarkets.

Oven temperatures

All oven temperatures in this book are listed for fan-forced ovens. If you don't have a fan-forced oven, raise the temperature by 20°C.

Panko breadcrumbs

Panko breadcrumbs are a Japanese-style breadcrumb that is super crunchy and tasty when fried. You will find these in most supermarkets.

Potato ricer

A potato ricer is a kitchen utensil used to mash potatoes by forcing them through small holes, typically about the diameter of a grain of rice. It is my favourite way to achieve super-smooth mashed potato.

Roux

Roux is flour and fat, typically butter, cooked together and used to thicken many sauces and gravies.

Stand mixer

A good stand mixer with a paddle, whisk and dough hook attachments will make baking a lot easier. If you don't have one, you can use a handheld electric mixer for all my recipes except for the bread-style doughs.

Yeast

Yeast is a rising agent. Believe it or not, it's actually live bacteria that eat the sugars in the dough and produce carbon dioxide as a byproduct, which is what makes bread rise. Yeast can be bought in a fresh or dried form, and you can find it at most delis. While I much prefer to use fresh yeast in my baking because I prefer the flavour, I have given you the option of choosing whichever one you'd prefer, mainly because dried yeast is more easily found. And I want to make it as easy as possible to get you baking! As a general rule, you need half the amount of dried yeast as you do fresh, but I've indicated this in all my recipes.

Gluten window

Index

C

D

E

S

T

Acknowledgements

To say writing this book is a dream come true would be an understatement. And I simply couldn't be where I am today without some very amazing people. What a wild ride these past ten years have been.

To my parents, Ellie and Mark, for always believing in me and supporting me no matter how crazy my ideas might be or how many arguments we have about them, I thank you. I simply wouldn't be the person I am today without both of you. I see all the hard work and sacrifices you've put in and made for me, and I will be forever thankful, even though sometimes I don't show it hahaha.

A big thanks to some of my first-ever stockists all those years ago for giving me the opportunity to get started, Rob Mauldon and Justin Beilin just to name a few. I'll never forget the doorway you helped open up in my life.

To my friend and mentor Lance Reynolds, your input is always highly valued and it's been a pleasure knowing you over the past four years, so thank you.

A huge thanks to my team at Bistro Morgan. A good business takes many great people, and I'm so proud of what we've built over the past seven years. Your energy and enthusiasm makes coming to work daily just that little bit better again.

To my amazing team who helped me put this book together, you guys are the best. To my publisher, Penguin Random House – Holly, Claire, Becca and Laura, thank you guys for believing in me. To my manager, Sarah, thank you for your organisational skills and your continuing support. To my friend and photoshoot chef John Sharkey, your energy in the kitchen over the course of the shoot was one of the main things that got me through those long days. To stylist Caroline Velik, thank you for making room in your busy schedule for me, especially at the last minute; it was so great working with you – you're truly a talent. And to photographer Elisa Watson, I don't think my food has ever looked so damn tasty!

And finally to you, the reader: thank you for allowing me to share my love and passion for food with the world. You've truly changed my life forever.

PENGUIN BOOKS

UK | USA | Canada | Ireland | Australia
India | New Zealand | South Africa | China

Penguin Random House Australia is part of the Penguin Random House group of companies whose addresses can be found at global.penguinrandomhouse.com.

First published by Penguin Books, an imprint of Penguin Random House Australia Pty Ltd, in 2021

Cover and text design by Rebecca King © Penguin Random House Australia Pty Ltd
Cover and internal photography by Elisa Watson
Photograph on page 9 (top left) by Chris Hillary; all other photographs on page 9 supplied by the author.
Food styling by Caroline Velik

Printed and bound in China

A catalogue record for this book is available from the National Library of Australia

ISBN 978 1 76 104384 0

Penguin Random House Australia uses papers that are natural and recyclable products, made from wood grown in sustainable forests. The logging and manufacture processes are expected to conform to the environmental regulations of the country of origin.

penguin.com.au